ANGER TURNED SIDEWAYS

ANGER TURNED SIDEWAYS

A HARTMANN

GIFT

Published by GIFT, Seattle

Edited and Designed by Girl Friday Productions
www.girlfridayproductions.com

Editorial: Ben Grossblatt
Cover and Interior Design: Rachel Christenson
Image Credits: Cover image © A Hartmann

ISBN-13: 9780998683003
eISBN: 9780998683010

First Edition

Printed in the United States of America

For everyone who believed in me.

CONTENTS

Anger turned inwards is depression.
Anger turned sideways is Hawkeye.

—Sidney Freedman (played by Allan Arbus),
*M*A*S*H*, season 5, episode 8

These fragments I have shored against my ruins . . .

—T. S. Eliot, *The Waste Land*

"NOT TO BE SOLD, RENTED, OR EXHIBITED WITHIN TWO HUNDRED MILES OF ST. LOUIS"

The Boy Scouts were a huge part of my life from the age of seven until twenty-two. Whatever you're thinking about the Scouts is almost certainly wrong. Norman Rockwell paintings aren't reality. What *is* reality is that by the age of fifteen I was tough, capable, and full of practical skills that most adults don't have at thirty. Leadership, public speaking, emergency preparedness. Most of my close friends in high school were also Eagle Scouts; it was normal in our circle.

Don't mistake this for adherence to any form of conservative social values. We were still teenage boys, albeit incredibly capable ones. The drinkers drank. The smokers smoked. The potheads got high. We all cursed like sailors. Our ability to organize, plan, and execute allowed us to get into a higher quality of trouble. It was the best pre-Internet way to obtain porn. Not to mention connections with our brethren on the other side of the legal fiction that is the "adulthood" line. Having a friend who knows that you won't rat them out for a carton of smokes, a case of beer, or a copy of *Hustler* goes a long way.

During my sophomore year in college, one of my younger friends was selected for the highest level of the honor camper society. Never mind the details—either you know what that is or the specifics don't matter. As his mentor I was instructed to make sure that he was at a Saturday morning pancake breakfast when he would be informed of this honor. Sean was a senior in high school and lived in a smaller city a half hour's drive north. The breakfast had been carefully timed for a weekend that was part of both the local high schools' and colleges' spring breaks (*spring* being a relative term given the amount of snow still on the ground in Wisconsin).

I was staying with family friends in the suburbs over the break, and my best friend and I decided to make the most of it. We'd both known Sean since he was a counselor-in-training at the camp we worked for. One of our other cohorts was also spending spring break with us, and the three of us vowed to give Sean a weekend he'd never forget and invited him down Friday night to stay with us.

Alcohol was drunk. Pot was smoked. Despite being clean and sober at the time, I remember very little of that Friday night. I recall doing a run for more frozen pizzas, as I was the only one in any shape to drive. Most importantly, no sleep was had.

There exist morning people; I've never approved of them. The award breakfast was set for 7:00 a.m. At 6:30 a.m. the four of us—all Eagle Scouts, all decorated for our achievements— got into our full Class A Scout uniforms, replete with sashes and pins, including uniform shorts and knee socks. We hadn't slept at all. I drove us to the church that was providing the space for the breakfast.

Possibly the less said about the breakfast, the better. Despite receiving an honor that is still significant to each of us, we were still jackass teenage boys.

It says a lot about the organization that they realized this kind of minor rebellion was not something to be crushed. We were still kids, we were blowing off steam, but they believed we were all good boys at heart. They didn't love that we showed up in various sorts of altered states, but our accomplishments at that tender age bought us a certain amount of good faith.

When we had finished breakfast, Sean was elated with his nomination for this high honor. As we headed back to the car, we realized we were a few blocks from Madison's largest adult bookstore and emporium. Some decisions aren't even conscious—the circumstances simply demand that they be made.

I drove us to the porn store. It didn't take five minutes.

"This is probably going to seem like a terrible idea later," I said while parking the car. "But we're already here."

"Um, guys? Problem," said Sean. "I'm still seventeen. They're going to card us, and I can't get in."

The other three of us shared a look and came to a silent consensus.

"Then you're going to have to wait in the car. We won't be too long. Here are the keys if you need to run the heater, but try not to run the battery down."

The clerk took our entry in his stride. He checked our IDs, but he probably would've even if we weren't in full Scout uniforms. We had legitimate identification, so he admitted us into the shop. We passed the glass cases of "tobacco pipes" and headed toward the porn.

If you're lucky, you've never asked yourself, "Who buys porn on a Saturday morning in the VHS era?" I assure you that you do not want to meet them. The sparse group of older men at first assumed we were some sort of morality police raid. Their confusion is understandable; clean-cut young men in uniforms are alarming. They became less tense when it was clear we were browsing for our own interests. Browsing mainly because we were destitute college students and couldn't afford to buy. I had three part-time jobs on campus, all suspended over the break. Cash was not something we had in any real quantity.

This lack of specie lead us to the discount table. Never, ever, check out the clearance table at an adult bookstore. It is by definition things that did not sell and no one wants. I'm not at all prudish now; even then I was fairly debauched. What's on the discount table is technically porn, but mostly sad. It's not the extreme things—it's the failures.

I picked up a video. "Not to be sold, rented, or exhibited within two hundred miles of St. Louis," read the notice on the back of the VHS box. It had been marked down to four dollars. I could afford it. I bought it. It bore the dubious title *Vicki's Revenge.*

Amazingly, in the Internet age I cannot find a copy or even proof this video ever existed.

If pornography is supposed to arouse or play to prurient interests, this was not it. The production was cheap; the set was obviously a fake living room backdrop, with a couple of couches. There was little, if any, erotic content. Neither of the women in it seemed enthusiastic about being there. The first half was one woman dominating the other, and the second featured a wrestling mat on the same set so they could "fight." The "revenge" mentioned in the title seems to refer to the woman dominated in the first half winning the catfight.

The last shot is of the face of the pinned woman, who starts crying. She says, "I'm not doing this," as the camera fades to black. The audio of her crying runs for another minute.

I left the tape behind when I moved after graduating. My successor apparently introduced it to our college's marching band. Since college marching bands are mostly fueled by cruelty, I'm told that it's become a tradition to watch it repeatedly.

BRANDED I

Like a lot of smart, aspiring pseudointellectual teenagers, I kept a journal, under the vain impression that my thoughts in adolescence were worth recording. Since I wasn't, say, hiding from fascists, surviving a shipwreck, or doing anything else of historic note, the journal was of course not very interesting. At best, parts of it may do a decent job of chronicling some of the particular facets of mental illness in a teenager, but most of it was fairly run-of-the-mill juvenile self-importance.

Except for one bit.

Inside the front cover of one of the notebooks I had drawn a design in a vaguely geometric style. It was just a sketch in black marker on a white surface. I must confess that like most of the rest of the contents, at fifteen I believed it to be deeply meaningful, but the design itself, stripped of any alleged meaning, remains striking. I have little talent and only a forced appreciation for the visual arts. I draw quite poorly and tend to be more interested in the history of a painting than its actual appearance, but to me the design had just the right balance of symmetry and asymmetry, and I remained enamored with it for the next couple of years.

Eventually I decided to have it tattooed on my left scapula when I turned eighteen. I could picture it perfectly: the design, the colors, the placement. It was going to be part of reaching the age of majority, and the placement was such that it could easily be concealed when I was dressed. The professions in which I aspired to work did not then really accept open displays of ink.

When I turned eighteen I decided that I was not making smart choices. A permanent mark, albeit a hidden one, seemed like a very bad idea. *Any* permanent idea seemed like a bad idea. I was self-aware enough to realize that I was making bad decisions, even if they were survivable ones, most of the time. Getting a tattoo was an extra complication I simply didn't need. I decided to wait until the next arbitrary milestone in American adult life and postponed the decision until I was twenty-one.

DRINKING THE KOOL-AID

By my junior year of high school we were allowed to start taking electives beyond the required curriculum. Although there were requirements for taking enough classes in some departments—Humanities, Math, Science—we were allowed a decent amount of latitude. This worked out well for me; I got to take a number of classes that were pleasantly outside my main academic interests. One particular favorite was Aerospace, a class devoted to learning the principles of aviation and preparing for pilot certification, a nice mix of physics and practical applications.

Another favorite class was Psychology. It was obviously a cursory introduction, lasting only a single term, but was an interesting class overall. While there was a healthy dose of regular topics like child development and Maslow's hierarchy, the real appeal of the class lay in the abnormal curriculum. The morbid fascination a lot of teenagers have with mental illness is a well-known phenomenon and is in part a way of dealing with the awkward stages of emotional development.

I am decreasingly sympathetic to this phenomenon as I get older.

I liked the class; unlike most of the students, I actually read the textbook assignments and took the course very seriously. My sincere interest in the field was not shared by a large portion of the students in my section.

To ameliorate the general lack of participation, the teacher did occasionally rely on more sensational efforts, most notably the 1980 miniseries *Guyana Tragedy: The Story of Jim Jones*, starring Powers Boothe. Due to its length, watching it took up four days of classroom time.

For those readers unfamiliar with the story, this is the short version: Jim Jones, a respected minister from Indiana who originally worked on civil rights and equality issues, moved to California, steadily went crazy, became a cult leader, took his entire congregation to Guyana, and in 1978 instigated a mass murder-suicide by drinking flavored water laced with cyanide. Contrary to popular myth, it was not Kool-Aid, but rather a generic knockoff. Still, the phrase "drink the Kool-Aid" is alternately traced back to this incident or to Ken Kesey spiking punch with LSD at counterculture parties in the sixties. Whatever the truth of its origins, the phrase obviously has negative connotations.

The connotations were good, however, for Powers Boothe, who won the Emmy for Outstanding Actor in a Limited Series or a Special in 1980 for his portrayal of Jim Jones.

By the end of the third classroom day of watching, the church had relocated to Guyana but had not yet completely lost touch with reality. This left me plenty of room to arrange a surprise for the fourth day and see who hadn't done the readings.

I had lunch scheduled right before Psych Class, which gave me freedom to move on my plan. That morning I'd brought to school a pitcher, a mixing spoon, a packet of grape beverage flavoring, a package of plastic cups, and a bottle of almond extract. I got ice water in the cafeteria, stirred in the drink mix, and then started pouring in the almond extract. Repeated tastings followed adding more extract until it was just slightly noticeable over the artificial grape flavor.

I set the pitcher and stack of plastic cups on a table near the entrance to the classroom and encouraged students to take a cup as they arrived. Some of the more diligent students declined, but none of them commented on the poor taste of the act or warned fellow students about it. It remains a mystery to me why the teacher let this proceed. The entire gesture was in incredibly bad taste. It's also possible she doubted my ability to source cyanide.

The rest of the class had some thoughts on the matter.

"This tastes a little funny, like there's a weird aftertaste."

I offered an insincere apology. "Sorry about that. It was a cheap generic that got thrown in for free with my groceries. Probably a little off."

"That's okay. Thanks for sharing anyway."

It was only about ten minutes into the lesson before the miniseries reached the "loyalty drills" that Jones conducted in the event the compound was raided. His followers were instructed to drink beverages that they believed were poisoned, and many complied, preferring death to persecution. The classroom began to murmur when they realized the cruel aftertastes of my actions.

Ten minutes later, the plot reached the point of cyanide poisoning. The class began to talk over the video openly. The teacher paused the video due to the classroom chatter.

"Gus, what was in the Kool-Aid?"

"Seriously, that's messed up, man."

"Don't worry about it. You're fine."

BRANDED II

As I started to become interested in computers I created the first electronic version of my logo. This was the first version to have color. The limitations of the tools at hand required these to be basic colors: red, light gray, and dark gray. In exactly those shades as defined by Pantone. Most computers of the day had limited color palettes for graphics, and with what little knowledge I had of design I made the colors easy to reproduce even with those rudimentary tools. I put this newly colorized version on my first webpage in the antediluvian year of 1995. A friend subsequently made it into a short animation: the design would grow and rotate until it was fully visible, then reverse itself and disappear again.

MARRIAGE ONE

It wasn't raining, but the mist was heavy, and the waterfall was throwing off an even heavier layer of moisture. From the observation pavilion at the top of the cliff, spotlights illuminated the whole scene: hundreds of feet of water cascading down the narrow gorge making a distant roar as it hit the water below.

I got down on one knee and produced the ring in its box. As she clasped her hands to her face, her surprise was immediate and explicit as I asked the question.

"Oh my god! Yes, yes!" she squealed with delight.

A chorus of "awww" could be heard behind us. A dozen teenage girls in formal dresses began applauding and crying behind us, their dates slightly more reserved but smart enough to at least show some enthusiasm for what the girls obviously thought was the most romantic moment they'd ever witnessed.

My now fiancée burst into tears herself. "I can't believe this is happening! My mother said the ring wasn't even done today!"

I hadn't planned that bit of collusion. Anna's mother, Joy, knew that it had been delivered because a family friend had done the custom setting for me, but she hadn't known that I'd picked that night to propose. Anna suspected something when I'd invited her to dress up nicely, not my usual style, but her mother had beautifully quashed her suspicions. I hadn't planned that it would be the night of a formal at the local high school. They say you should never propose unless you already know the answer will be positive, but my proposal went better than I could have hoped.

We both spent the next year planning an incredibly elaborate wedding and developing increasingly cold feet. At the same time as her mother's health began to decline, Anna increasingly returned to the fundamentalist Christianity of her upbringing. Joy was the only real family she had, and Anna relied more and more on prayer as the prognosis worsened. Our nominal involvement with the megachurch escalated to more frequent attendance and volunteering for various projects and events.

Our lives became a series of simple routines. We stopped going out dancing. Our weekends became ordinary dates of dinner at chain restaurants and movies by major studios. Movies are an excellent way to have dates in which a couple do not need to make eye contact or speak with one another while maintaining the illusion that quality time is being shared. And all the time the wedding plans continued to expand: a dove release, ice sculptures, hunting for the perfect chapel, a three-week honeymoon in Fiji. We took the premarital counseling the megachurch required.

The pressure was intense; even prior to her mother's downturn Anna had become frantic from stage-managing what had turned into an elaborate pageant. Every detail was elaborately choreographed, down to which "spontaneous" pictures the photographer should take. I was not to wear my glasses during the ceremony or in any of the pictures, as that was not how Anna wanted to remember the day. We were locked in a game of wedding chicken with neither of us wanting to admit that we were both growing uneasy and that we knew we were wrong for each other by that point.

The week before the wedding itself was frantic. All the preparations required huge amounts of attention. Anna's mother had flown in early, nominally to help, but once she was here her condition deteriorated substantially. She looked like a wraith, pale and emaciated. On the Tuesday before the wedding she checked herself into a local hospital.

Against doctor's orders Joy checked herself out of the hospital the day before the wedding so she could attend the rehearsal dinner. She looked even worse than she had earlier in the week. It was clear that she was now operating on raw willpower in order to live until her daughter's wedding.

I showed up at the wedding, said my lines, had the right pictures taken, and went to the reception. It was a beautifully executed farce. At the end of the night we retired to the suite we'd rented for the night, and we departed for Fiji the next day.

Fiji was beautiful; we spent most of our honeymoon on a small island entirely owned by a hotel that never had more than two dozen guests. All of us were couples; most of us were honeymooners. We were completely cut off from the world. There was a single phone on the island, in the main office, and Internet access and cell phone coverage were nonexistent. The only news I could get was secondhand reports from one of the hotel workers, who would relay updates from the BBC short-wave. I heard about the Seattle WTO riots while lying on a beach half a world away.

Our return flight had a connection in Los Angeles, the first time we were reachable. Upon turning on our cell phones, we were both inundated with voice mail notifications. The news was not good. On her return to Dallas, Anna's mother had gone straight to the hospital and asked her lawyer to redraft her will and health care directive. Anna spoke with her mother by phone, and Joy sounded heavily medicated. They talked for most of the layover, and as soon as we landed in Seattle we immediately made arrangements for Anna to fly to Dallas as soon as possible. I would follow as soon as I could arrange additional pet sitting and let work know that there had been an emergency.

The following two days were pretty bad. Joy had lost consciousness by the time Anna reached Dallas. Some friends of the family kept calling me to share updates as they happened. Joy was only being kept alive by life support, and the doctors were certain there was no hope left, but they were hesitant to inform Anna before I arrived. I made the necessary arrangements in Seattle to handle a longer absence and obtained a bereavement-fare flight to Dallas. I was met at the airport by family friends and taken directly to the hospital. One of the doctors and a grief counselor took us into a small room they use to break bad news to families. There was no hope, and they needed our consent to remove the ventilator. Anna was devastated. I went emotionally numb. We waited what felt like an eternity in the grieving room. Eventually we were taken to Joy. At the brunch the morning after the wedding she had looked bad; now she looked even worse. It was obvious that all the medical equipment connected to her body was the only thing keeping her alive.

Euphemism lies. The plug is not actually pulled, nor is a relative the one who turns things off. Once the order is signed, the attending physician removes the hydration IV and shuts down the ventilator, and there is a brief, terrible period while the body accepts the end has come. We held her hands while the life went out of her body. And then it was over. We cried. They declared time of death.

Funeral preparations were made. It is standard practice to identify the body at the funeral home to ensure that no mistakes were made in the transfer from the hospital's morgue. Thankfully this does not require seeing the actual body, only a picture. I did this so Anna didn't have to have that as her last view of her mother. The face on the Polaroid was just familiar enough for me to identify. As W. Somerset Maugham wrote, "The dead look so terribly dead when they're dead."

There were some interesting surprises while processing the estate. I found several books on how to get a false degree, calling into question some of Joy's earlier careers. The court had trouble probating the will, as *Joy* turned out not to be her legal name. Despite appearing on her driver's license, it did not appear on her birth certificate or passport. In the innocence of the pre-9/11 era, she was able to get a driver's license with her baptismal certificate. To make things more complicated, her friends were unable to testify as to her actual legal name.

We closed accounts, collected valuables too important to leave with movers, and prepared the house to go on the market. The small natural gas prospecting company she owned was sold to her former business partner. We dealt with the life insurance company. The dog was given to the friends who had been caring for her when Joy's illness had become too much.

After we had made the most urgent preparations, we packed up the car and set out for Seattle with two cats, as many of Joy's guns as we could find in the house, the critical valuables, and the most important legal papers.

The drive back to Seattle, and to the start of our married life, was a haze of sad cats and highway hypnosis. We ate Christmas dinner in a depressing buffet restaurant in Albuquerque across the street from our Holiday Inn Express.

It was not a good portent for a marriage.

BRANDED III

In college I continued to develop the idea of having a logo. In part this was due to my increased interest in music, album art, and band logos. At the time, I read an interview with Trent Reznor about how he'd selected the name Nine Inch Nails for his band. He said essentially that it abbreviated well and could easily have a cool logo. There were also the often-mocked attempt by Prince to change his name to a glyph, which, actually, he'd been using as a logo for years, and any number of other bands with easily drawn and instantly recognizable logos. Many of these are so iconic in popular culture that they require no further explanation.

In a similar vein I began to read more about Peter Saville, the graphic designer for Factory Records and for legendary bands like Joy Division and New Order. He'd decided early on to minimize explanations and let the art itself be the only explanation. On some of the albums he designed, even the band name was omitted from the packaging. It was the idea of an open secret as a brand. If the viewer knew what it was, they felt like they were in on a secret, even if it was a secret shared with millions of people. This was tremendously appealing to me.

I began to think of myself as a brand.

THREE RANDOM MOMENTS ABOUT FERTILITY

1. PATERNITY

"Welcome to fatherhood, fucker!" was the subject line of the e-mail. I was sipping my coffee while sitting in the pale morning light of spring, reading my personal e-mail to wake myself up. Taken aback, I read it again. Still the same e-mail, from the same recent ex-girlfriend. I went into a mild panic—the same feeling that for centuries men have had when greeted with that news.

Breathing deeply and now gulping the coffee as though enough caffeine could make this go away, I opened the message. "How could you do this to me?" was alongside "You'll never know this baby," juxtaposed with "You bastard, you've ruined my life."

.

Too much awake and anxious, I called my best friend. It was earlier than we usually spoke, but he answered right away. Fatherhood does funny things to a man.

"Hello?"

"It's me. Something important is happening." Tangible panic in my voice.

"Hey! Take a deep breath. What's going on?" We'd been friends for a decade, since college; these calls have sometimes meant death, layoffs, divorce, disaster. We'd weathered it all.

"Savannah says she's pregnant and I'm the father."

A pause. He was clearly thinking it over.

"You broke up with her because she was crazy, remember? She took it pretty hard. She called up our house the other night to try to make friends with us separately."

"I'm so sorry. God! Do you think this is just part of her craziness?"

"Buddy, you and I both know it is."

"I just wish I could be sure."

"It'll be okay. Just get checked to make sure it didn't accidentally reverse."

2. VIRILITY

The fertility clinic insisted that all men were most potent between six and eight in the morning. I had a small argument with the receptionist; I was nearly nocturnal as a student, and my nervous system was long accustomed to my selected lifestyle. It was a fruitless endeavor, and at 6:30 a.m. I was riding my motorcycle through the cold February morning, and it was barely light. Under my leathers I was shivering, wondering if this was the right choice.

It was nice to get inside the hospital complex; state-run steam heat at least made it feel as though life should exist there. However, the postwar monstrosity of a building made finding the clinic a challenge—every department was a hexagon-shaped "module," and I had to hunt through the dozen or so towers to find the correct eighth floor. I found it, eventually, wincing at the OB/GYN sign on the door almost instinctively. Old habits die hard.

The receptionist, overly perky for such an early hour, found my name on the schedule and called the project coordinator. She came to the lobby to meet me.

"Hi, Gus? I'm Lauren." She didn't offer to shake hands. "Can you please come with me?" She gestured back down the maze of hallways off the lobby.

"It's nice to meet you. Sure, let's go." Carrying my helmet and saddlebags did make me feel a bit awkward, but not too much. After all, I had answered their ad and been accepted.

Lauren lead me through a few turns of the hallway, all the 120-degree turns of the beehive, and not the right angles of the Cartesian, eventually arriving in a cramped office covered in files, paperwork, and other administrivia. Finding some sort of desk amid the detritus, Lauren stepped behind it and gestured me to a seat on the other side. She plucked a file off the top of a pile, tagged with my name in large block capitals.

"Okay, it looks like your phone screen went fine. I just need you to sign this form confirming what you told us." I read the form. An abridged list of what I promised: that I wasn't a drug user; that my family had no history of heart disease, strokes, cancer, or diabetes; that I wasn't a homosexual; that I had never had a homosexual experience.

I signed it. None of it was really any of their business.

"Great! Well, here's your collection jar." She produced a large glass container from underneath the desk, the word *sterile* in bold letters on the tape sealing the jar. It bore an uncanny resemblance to the glasses tall drinks were served in at my favorite bar.

"Um, okay. And I should take this where?"

"Oh, there's a men's room off the lobby."

"A men's room?"

"Is that a problem for you?"

A generation of humor on this topic had given me a rather different image: a private room, with a light over the door labeled Do not enter when light is on. But leaving comedy behind, I figured they were the professionals.

"No, that's fine. Can I leave my motorcycle stuff here in the meantime?" I gestured with my helmet, displaying its bulk.

"Um, could you just keep all your stuff with you? We really can't be responsible for anything you leave here." Lauren gave me a weak smile, as though these weren't her rules.

I didn't even think about it for a minute.

"No, that's fine. Which way back to the lobby?" I stood up, and Lauren smiled again and pointed to the left of her office door. I smiled back as a reflex, and trudged back to where I had come in.

The men's room was actually outside the lobby; it was attached to the adjacent hallway. I silently cursed television for all the untruths it had told me about this experience and pushed the door open, stopping just inside to look for a lock on the door so I wouldn't be interrupted.

There was no lock on the door.

My heart skipped a beat, and I sighed. I hung my saddle-bags and jacket on the coatrack by the door and placed my helmet atop the attached shelf. I picked the middle of the three stalls.

I sighed again as I latched the stall door and gazed at the intimidating bottle.

3. STERILITY

"Are you sure you want to do this?" asked the surgeon. "You have to think of this as permanent; reversals aren't always possible."

The paper covering the vinyl tabletop crinkled as I raised my head to look at him. "I'm sure," I said. "I'm very sure." I laid my head back down so I couldn't see the surgical drape covering me from the waist down.

"Okay, then. The local should have taken effect, but this is still going to hurt."

I turned my head to the right, eyes closed, and bit my tongue right as the scalpel pierced my skin. Feeling the pain only as something very far away, I smiled.

THE END OF THE BEGINNING

My first wife and I never really recovered from the rough first month of our marriage. We both pretended everything was okay, but by our first anniversary it was clear to everyone around us that we weren't happy. It took our first significant time apart for us to see it too.

My first visit to a strip club came while I was at a technical conference in New Orleans. I'd never been to a club before, and the general theme of debauchery in the Big Easy combined with the tail end of a pretty tough year made it seem like an excellent idea. This was the same week that I started drinking; I'd reconsidered my childhood decision to stay sober. No better place or time.

Since it was my first real drinking experience, my friends who were in attendance decided to keep an eye on me. Matt, in particular, decided to double-pace my drinking, since he could gauge when he was drunk, and if I had only had half that, I'd be okay.

Bourbon Street isn't to my tastes today. It's too much like "amateur drinking night" when lots of people who don't normally go on a bender take the opportunity. The problem is that they are unpredictable. Until one has been off the leash enough, one's response is always unpredictable. As was mine on that first trip.

When a group of four guys in their midtwenties arrives at a New Orleans strip club, it is not noteworthy. It becomes noteworthy a couple of hours later when one of the group is clearly throwing money around, buying all the drinks, and obviously being protected by the rest of the group. I still remember the dancer who gave me my first table dance there; for legal reasons at least one foot had to remain on the small table in the booth. She had a tattoo of the scales of justice as a full back piece, and when I complimented it she demurred and said it needed more work.

On the second night one of the dancers asked if I was in a band. They couldn't figure out how a guy in a well-worn army surplus jacket could be throwing money around while protected by an entourage. There was significant money, but we were young, not particularly clean cut, and obviously not used to that kind of money. Later the same night they started changing the music to suit my tastes in midnineties industrial more often than not. Clearly we were lucrative customers and worth indulging.

On the third night, the DJ actually changed the song in the middle when we walked into the club. The dancer on stage wasn't thrilled about it, but as I would learn years later, internal club politics are complicated, and the dancers don't want any conflict with the DJ. Better to dance to a song you don't like once than get on the DJ's bad side. I didn't realize at the time that Bourbon Street clubs don't normally play goth/industrial music.

She was bleach-blonde and lithe. I tipped her on stage, as I'd been liberally throwing bills all night. After her stage show, she came by to see if I wanted a table dance. I did, and we ended up in a booth in back with the nominal table left unused. I mentioned to her that I usually go for gothy girls, and suddenly she pulled out a few hairpins from the shock-blonde wig to reveal black hair that she then shook free. We spent a while together in the booth, interacting well beyond even what the laws of New Orleans allow. She told me a story about a bad night with an abusive boyfriend and claimed that after he hit her she broke his arm with a fireplace poker before coming to work. I'd already been buying her drinks before she told me that she'd dropped a major downer to avoid thinking about going home to her abusive boyfriend.

She asked if she could come back to my hotel with me. I agreed, even if it meant kicking Matt out of our double room. I knew he'd understand.

The DJ announced that she was next on stage. There's a rotation for stage performers; it's part of the normal operation at a club. Stage shows are at best an advertisement for private dances and at worst a chance to get stiffed on tips by men at the rail. I asked her not to go, offered to pay whatever house fee or DJ bribe was needed. This wasn't generosity, more a desperate attempt to have her remain in contact with me. She refused, and with a booze- and pill-fueled bravado she told me she wanted to show me her pole acrobatics. After a kiss, she asked me what song I wanted. I named one of my favorites.

I gave her a hug, and as she headed to the stage I headed to the tip rail. My friends headed there too, all of us with drinks in hand.

Her acrobatics were actually amazing, particularly given her state. She was doing something complicated at the top of the pole when she suddenly lost all muscle control and dropped to the floor. The housemother ran out to check on her. The song ended, and as the DJ forgot to change discs, a familiar morose song started to play. "Took a lot to live a lot like you."

"Everybody out!" shouted the bouncer. The dancer was still lying askew on the stage; no one had moved her for fear of spinal injury. We got up and left, too startled even to take our to-go drinks that are a staple of New Orleans. The club patrons spilled out onto Bourbon Street.

My friend Tyson and I waited outside, watched the ambulance come, and saw her hauled out on a backboard, still unconscious.

I found out later she was okay and limp enough when she fell to not get hurt despite the unpleasant *cracking* sound when she hit the floor. Asking about her condition the next day was apparently unexpected by the club staff; I'm not sure if they were more surprised that I'd shown up again after such a bad experience or that I seemed sincerely interested in her well-being. Perhaps it was unusual to be humanized in a business where both sides dehumanize one another.

BRANDED IV

The next major milestone came during my first *intermatrium*, the period between my first divorce and second marriage. A decade since initially wanting the symbol as a tattoo, with a series of lapses along the way, I decided that it was finally time. I printed out a hard copy of the design and approached a local tattoo parlor that had good reviews and, nearly as importantly, was a mere two blocks from my best friend's place. The artist listened to my idea, took the hard copy, and told me to come back in a week, when he'd have a sketch ready. Due to the curve of the scapula, it's nontrivial to make the finished design *look* straight and correct while working with the topography of the human body. The finished sketch looked a bit crooked on paper, but once the stencil was applied, along with a layer of deodorant, which apparently can help ink transfer from tissue paper, the pattern on my back was exactly what I wanted. The tattooing itself took a little over an hour and was not as painful as people seem to believe. I was now officially, and more or less indelibly, marked.

VAX 11/785

"Goddamn it, push harder! The traffic light's going to change!"

"What are they going to do, hit us? This thing weighs a ton. Their car would take much more damage than this thing would."

"That doesn't help us, does it, asshole?"

We had to shout to be heard over the usual noise of traffic and the marked increase of car horns caused by our presence. We were four scruffy college students pushing something the size of an industrial refrigerator across a public street at rush hour, screwing up an already bad place to commute.

"Fuck, the casters are too small to go up the sidewalk ramp!"

"Push!" one voice replied.

"Just push!" a second said.

Most people are vaguely aware that computers used to be physically large machines but tend to think of it as a long time ago. In fact, some computers are still big. They've become increasingly rare, and they were already pretty rare when we were given this one. It had been found by one of our troupe as a dust-covered discard in a back hallway of the Engineering building of our university. This one was somewhere around six feet wide by six feet high by three feet deep. It'd been a powerful machine in its day for doing advanced modeling but had long since been overtaken by newer and smaller technologies. It had been relegated to a hallway, waiting to be scrapped.

Ownership of the hardware, the main module and two appliance-sized external pieces, changed hands in a bland 1950s office, decades out of date. The representative of the College of Engineering, the current owners, was less than certain about our delegation of young men. Today we would be suspected of wanting the copper to buy meth: lean, hungry, and ready to jump on an opportunity to steal something ostensibly valuable.

He coughed in a way only a university bureaucrat can cough. "So you"—cough—"gentlemen represent an official arm of the Computer Sciences department?"

"I'm not sure that's exactly the term, sir. We're both an officially sanctioned student organization, and we belong to a special project of Professor Johnson's that allows undergraduates unprecedented access to computing resources. He's been running the projects lab for the last decade or so and has obtained us hardware grants from industry partners. He's even secured us our own office space in the Comp Sci building."

"I see. Is Professor Johnson unavailable to come ask for this equipment himself?"

"He's spending a semester guest-lecturing at the University of California, Berkeley, where he did his doctorate. In his absence, you can contact the director of the Systems—"

He waved his hand. This had clearly met the level of deniability he wanted.

"That thing goes, and it never comes back to the College of Engineering, understand? It's Comp Sci's problem now. We've looked into getting rid of it, and all the gold and copper in it won't cover disposal. Just get it out of here."

He handed us the keys. That generation of computer required real keys to open and move them.

As cited above, we rallied our manpower to get it the four blocks to our lab in the Computer Science building. Those "fucks" and "assholes" were only the tip of the iceberg of vulgarities; many further shouted obscenities and discussions about matters of physics followed. Many conversations involved both.

"Fucking mechanical advantage says we go *sideways zigzag* up the ramp!"

"You have no idea what that term even means! We get a block and tackle and use pulleys to get it up the ramp!"

"How the fuck do we get one of those?"

I refuse to name names, but I maintain that a group of underweight engineering students should have figured out mechanical advantage better.

Once we had the computer safely in our clutches, the folly of having acquired the whole system finally became apparent. We lacked the amount of electricity to power it, even if the computing power was worth having. Ownership of it constituted a substantial detriment in almost every possible way. It was heavy, electrically demanding, computationally weak, and nearly entirely obsolete. So we did something we were uniquely qualified to do as the bottom-feeders of the local tech community.

We gutted it. A swarm of students with tools removed every screw, pulled every circuit board, removed every microchip. Jackals and vultures don't begin to bring to mind how thoroughly we gutted it. Parts that had any use were salvaged; those that didn't were dissected into even smaller pieces. It was the mechanical equivalent of butchering a whale on a beach. The entire process took days, some of us staying the whole time, powered by youth and excessive amounts of Jolt Cola and

SURGE. The end result was a fantastic emptied chassis, several huge piles of screws, microchips, computer boards, actually useful components, and at least a dozen exhausted students.

Ultimately we made good use of much of it. The useful parts were traded for favors to the professionals in the department. The obsolete microchips were used to create a beautiful swirling design on the ceiling of our lab, lovingly pressed into the acoustic tiling. The cabinet itself made a wonderful bookshelf once we'd tired of seeing how many students we could fit inside of it at a time. The cooling fans were pressed into service for drying carpet after a wet cleaning. The screws ended up in a cookie jar that we would use for whatever projects we were building.

The cabinet itself lived on for at least another decade holding the lab's books, the microchip ceiling art at least that long. The sheer folly of the exploit lasted in oral tradition well beyond any of our times at the university.

BRANDED V

I absolutely loved—and still love—my first tattoo. But it was of limited use in actually promoting my brand to anyone who hadn't seen me shirtless. Mesh shirts weren't uncommon in those days, but again only a fairly small group of people would have seen me in one.

I decided to pursue something that could be distributed easily and indiscriminately, so the unit cost had to be fairly low. I settled on business cards. There is no end of printers that can make them, so the market is very competitive, and the social protocol of handing out cards has a long enough history to be ubiquitous. The custom of handing out personal cards as a form of introduction was emerging again around the time I was considering my next move. I wanted to continue the idea of a secret brand, so the logo, in full color, was the entire front of the card while the back was left blank. This *tabula rasa* allowed me to determine arbitrarily how much information I wanted to provide or whether, as frequently happened, to provide no information at all. I would occasionally leave blank copies with the fliers for upcoming concerts or club nights. Patrons of such nightclubs are used to rifling through the papers on offer, and on numerous occasions I saw people pick up one of my cards with the others, flip it over looking for more information, and become confused at the empty space presented to them. Other times I would write my name and contact info on the back and, on a few occasions, false information.

I should probably be more ashamed of that.

UNDER THE GUN

Growing up, even the idea of guns was controversial in my home. I didn't grow up with guns, not even toy guns. My mother told some sort of story about a thankfully nonfatal incident involving her older sister finding my grandfather's gun and, for some reason, shoving a bullet up her nose. This sounds like bullshit to me, but such is family lore.

Because of the lore, it was a huge break to even get to own G.I. Joe figures. Not the original twelve-inch ones from the sixties—the smaller reincarnation in the eighties. My mother's aversion to firearms ran so deep that apparently even a toy with a tiny gun was a problem, as it might make firearms seem a normal part of life.

As a young man, my father had been an avid marksman. He'd earned a varsity letter in riflery in New York City, back when a teenager with a gun at school seemed harmless. He'd shot competitively with the Scouts. He didn't hunt. I think he had one of the most reasonable understandings of firearms in America. They exist, they're fun in a safe environment, and they are for sport only.

When I was seven, I badly wanted the toy knife with the spring-loaded, retractable plastic blade that was sold at the local discount store. The problem was that it came with an equally fake toy pistol, which was unacceptable to my mother. This lead to what later as an adult I realized was a proxy battle between my parents about larger, more fundamental issues about their differing approaches to childrearing. Eventually some sort of deal had been brokered that allowed the set to be purchased so long as I wasn't given the fake gun. I was happy to get the fake knife and wasn't overly upset about not getting the gun.

My father gave it to me about two months after I was given the knife. He gave it to me in the garage where his workbench was and told me not to tell my mother. I was grateful and excited at the time. It's only creepy in retrospect that they were keeping parenting decisions from one another.

It's kind of a fluke that I first shot a rifle around the time my parents got divorced. My first summer at Boy Scout camp included getting to shoot .22LR rifles, which proved amazingly fun. The following fall my father set me up with a local gun club, which had a juniors' division for competitive target riflery. He had his competition rifle from high school refurbished, and despite being thirty-five years old, it was in perfect mechanical shape.

To anyone inexperienced with firearms, competition guns are the exact opposite of the guns known as "assault weapons." My competition rifle weighs eighteen pounds, can only fire a single shot at a time without manually cycling the action, and has the longest and heaviest barrel allowed by competition rules. It's precise at a certain range, but it's unwieldy, heavy, and slow. It shoots a caliber that isn't fit for hunting anything but vermin. In short, it is a firearm made for competition, not violence. I still own it. If it were a person, my rifle would be eligible for a pension at this point.

I enjoyed shooting competitively, even though that heavy a gun was a bit tough for a ten-year-old. It was nice to do that with my father once a week. I came home from the local National Guard armory reeking of gunpowder; I assume my mother only failed to notice because of her infatuation with her new husband.

I had no common ground with the other youth shooters. While we'd wait for range time, sitting in the common area, we'd try to talk. A sixteen-year-old who was a crack shot was doing his homework, reading at a fourth-grade level at best. Others of the kids were smart but rural; I was from a bedroom community with parents who'd grown up in cities. Unlike in the Scouts, I had no friends there. I have no idea what they thought of me.

I shot with them for a couple of years, completing some achievements. Then my interest in guns kind of faded away for about a decade.

Moving out West was surprising. There were basically no gun laws in Washington State when I arrived. In point of fact, there were laws prohibiting more restrictive laws. Only in 2014 was the personal sale of unregistered guns without paperwork made illegal. Which is to say, I could sell a handgun to any-one without a background check, and we would not legally be required to report it. Voters passed the ballot initiative against substantial opposition.

I joined a gun club within the first year of moving to Seattle. For the first fifteen years I was in Washington, this member-ship allowed me to buy and sell firearms freely at gun shows with other members. Commercial dealers were required to perform instant federal background checks over the phone, private individuals were not. The distinction had nothing to do with the number of guns on offer; some private collectors operating as individuals had more stock than smaller licensed stores. The best way to differentiate the two is if the price tag says plus tax on it; commercial dealers charge sales tax and were the only ones required to perform background checks.

I didn't buy from the commercial dealers much. Why create a paper trail that isn't required? I like gaming any system's rules.

At twenty-three I bought a Glock 19, a nine-millimeter semiautomatic pistol, partially because I was a soft-left individual politically and it was a very antithetical thing to do for my general beliefs. A few months later I bought what the press would call an AK-47, because journalists know little about guns and a lot about headlines. The rifle is properly called the Maadi MISR, and while cosmetically similar to the AK, it only fires once per pull on the trigger. It was mostly made in Egypt with enough American parts to slide through the massive loopholes of the 1994 Assault Weapons Ban.

That those were my first two firearm purchases was not a coincidence. I liked the idea of buying guns with undeserved bad reputations. The perversity and subversion amused me. It seemed provocatively in poor taste.

From the day they were introduced, Glocks were denounced as plastic guns that would foil airport security and be a linchpin of terrorism. This mythos was passed on by the blockbuster film *Die Hard 2*, which claimed the existence of a Glock 7 that was allegedly made of porcelain. No such gun has ever existed, from Glock or any other manufacturer. In fact, there is a significant amount of metal in every model Glock that will trigger every security system. Civilian models of rifles derived from the Kalashnikov, while superficially identical to *actual* AK-47s, were penalized for being well-designed semiautomatic rifles. In fact, they're no different from Remingtons and Winchesters sold for hunting. They just look evil in popular culture after two decades of movie villains and news footage of terrorists carrying similar things.

The same year I also bought several items from the NYPD gift shop. In the pre-9/11 era, the public could still criticize the NYPD for excessive force, disproportionately killing minorities, or sodomizing an innocent suspect with a foreign object in a precinct bathroom before he even got to see a lawyer. I bought gear to be in deliberate bad taste when "bad taste" was still funny. Culture jamming at its finest.

I still own guns. I barely use them anymore, even at the range. I never carry them despite Washington's laws and a national conservative political movement encouraging me to do so. There is not a chance, to use the euphemism of the violent, that I'd "stand my ground" and execute some random maybe-assailant.

I don't love guns. The history, the science, the engineering, some of the pop culture, I love academically. If I moved to a country that has more sensible gun laws tomorrow, I'd be fine melting down my entire collection.

Except for maybe my father's rifle. It'd be nice to pass that down to someone.

BRANDED VI

I was happy with the business cards, and the overall success led me to consider other merchandise. Small and cheap were once again the ideal attributes for something to be handed out, but I was looking for something more useful to people. The cards got attention but would then vanish into obscurity more often than not. Something with a practical purpose was needed, and I brainstormed ideas for months. I rejected several possibilities for cost or feasibility: custom pens lack adequate surface area to display the logo; notepads are both expensive to have made and somewhat odd to hand to a casual acquaintance. I finally settled on an item commonly found in bars and nightclubs at the time: matchbooks. Picking up a matchbook from a bar or table is a common occurrence even for nonsmokers. Writing inside a paper matchbook is another classic trope, something straight out of noir films. I decided to pursue matchbooks as my new merchandise.

This proved to be a fool's errand. Custom matchbooks come in two quantities: short-run batches for special events like weddings and larger runs designed for restaurants or bars. The former has a very high unit cost; the latter has a much lower unit cost but a minimum order of roughly one hundred times larger than the small batch, usually somewhere in the thousands. There are a number of federal regulations about matchbooks, from restricted shipping due to the incendiary nature to required contact information provided on each book. The latter explicitly contradicted my goal of not providing information, but I was prepared to possibly have a post office box if necessary. However, the killing blow was delivered by a measure I supported: the Washington State indoor smoking ban passed by popular vote in 2005. Suddenly the idea of distributing something most commonly associated with smoking seemed anachronistic. I abandoned my quest for matchbooks.

No new ideas came to me for another couple of years, partially because I'd eliminated all the things I had originally thought of, and partially because I was busy with a new job. Brand promotion remained in the background, mainly limited to handing out my cards with contact info and occasionally minor bathroom graffiti in the kinds of bars that encourage that sort of thing. There are, fortunately, many of those in my neighborhood. One establishment in particular had at one point no fewer than six instances of my logo scratched into the plastic faux brickwork. These were at best half measures that left me dissatisfied. I wanted another option.

A: MY TRIP TO OMAHA. Q: WHAT IS A WASTED JOURNEY?

I was seventeen. My mother had decamped for Florida, and I was living by myself. My father and older sister were still in Madison, but we'd reached a status quo where leaving me to my own devices was just easiest for everyone. I went to school, had a part-time job, and was active in the Boy Scouts, and I behaved well enough to be left alone.

I'd forgotten having sent in the postcard by the time the invitation arrived in October. *Teen Jeopardy* tryouts for my region would be the first weekend of November in Omaha, a little over four hundred miles from Madison. They would be held at a large downtown hotel. I had the option of a Friday or Sunday session and just needed to present my invitation letter to be admitted.

This was a tremendously exciting prospect. I was a smart kid, reliably good at trivia and puzzles, and had no fear about public speaking. It seemed obvious that this was an opportunity I had to seize. Planning all the driving, it looked as though by leaving Saturday afternoon and spending the night in Des Moines, I'd reach Omaha early enough for the tryouts. There was the minor matter of not being old enough to get a motel room, but I persuaded my absent mother to arrange one for me. My friend Lawrence offered to come along to split the driving, and we left Madison as a light snow was beginning to fall.

Most of the clichés about driving through Iowa are true. The road was flat and straight. The cornfields were barren in winter. We arrived in Des Moines without incident and checked into the motel. I'm not sure that any reputable establishment today would admit two seventeen-year-olds based on a phone call from an adult they'd never seen.

Sunday morning was sunny and beautiful. We got an early start and hit the interstate in my pickup truck. At the rate we were traveling we would easily make Omaha in time for lunch and before the tryouts.

Forty-nine miles outside of Omaha, where I-80 intersects State Route 59, my truck ground to a halt. All the lights on the dashboard were lit. The power steering and brakes were gone, and I had to fight to get the truck onto the shoulder of the highway. The engine was dead and wouldn't restart. There was just a sad grinding noise when I turned the ignition.

Grabbing our luggage, we headed up the highway embankment to a gas station in search of a pay phone. The clerk didn't like the look of us; two long-haired teenagers from out of town carrying duffel bags gave the impression of being either runaways or low-grade weed dealers.

·

"Can I help you boys?"

I took point. "My truck broke down just past the off-ramp. Do you have a phone I can use?"

"There's a pay phone back by the bathrooms."

"Toll-free calls are still free from it, right? I just have to call AAA and get a tow."

This seemed to legitimize us in his eyes. We might be miscreants, but at least we were determined to keep moving out of his town. After AAA had towed my car to the station, he let us try to solicit a ride to Omaha from customers stopping for gas.

"Pardon me, sir, but are you headed into Omaha? Our car broke down, and we're trying to get to the Greyhound station to get home."

"Ma'am, we're students with car trouble. Is there any way you could give us a ride into Omaha so we can catch a bus home?"

"Excuse me, sir, but our car's broken down, and we're just trying to get to Omaha so we can get a Greyhound back to school."

This series of entreaties went on for hours. Sometimes the receiving party would look at the clerk, who'd gesture to my truck in the parking lot and shrug, as that was all of my story he knew to be true.

After two hours, the cashier had reached the end of his shift and offered to drive us into Omaha for gas money. It was most of the rest of our cash, but it was still a ride, and I wasn't going to turn it down. We got to the Red Lion just in time for my *Teen Jeopardy* tryout.

Phase One of the tryout process was a timed video test: sixty of us in the hotel's general-purpose convention room, all trying to keep up with a rapid-fire series of questions coming from the TV and writing out all our answers longhand. They were all in the classic *Jeopardy* format of announcing a category before providing the "answer." Thankfully we were not expected to write out the answers in the form of questions. It was very easy to fall behind.

I can't speak to Phase Two at all. Only two people out of our group of sixty passed Phase One. It was a bitter disappointment, having come that far and at that cost to get nothing. We weren't told our scores; the MC had some rather condescending advice that we just tell anyone asking that we "almost made it." We were dismissed, and Lawrence and I found ourselves in the lobby of the hotel with no transport plan and no money.

The least worst plan was to collect-call my father and get Greyhound tickets wired. Since my father wasn't aware that I'd crossed multiple state lines as a minor, we came up with a reasonably plausible lie; we jumped Lawrence's life ahead a year, making him eighteen and a college freshman. This was shockingly easy to do, as his plans were already fairly set. He was going to attend the University of Wisconsin and declare his major in chemistry, but continue living at home. The last bit being particularly relevant in the event that he needed to get dropped off when we reached Madison. My father was not happy about the situation but agreed to have the tickets waiting at the Omaha bus station with the understanding that I would have to pay him back.

The Greyhound station in Omaha was a pretty sketchy place for two teenage boys, and we had several hours to wait. We spent a lot of time trying to stick together and generally be invisible. Things were marginally better once we were on the bus, which was fortunate because we were on the bus for a very long time. Unsurprisingly there is no direct route from Omaha to Madison; the shortest route involves transferring in Chicago, continuing north to Milwaukee, and then cutting back west to reach Madison. The total duration of the bus trip was roughly double the direct-driving time. The first leg to Chicago was an overnight run; we took turns sleeping fitfully and arrived somewhat the worse for wear. It was midday before we made it back to Madison, and my father picked us up at the bus station. I introduced him to Lawrence, who declined a ride and took the bus home.

We then set about the business of getting my truck shipped back. The town I'd broken down in was just big enough to have its own Chevy dealership, which was able to get the truck from the garage where AAA had left it. The service department checked it out, and the prognosis was not good. The engine had thrown a rod and was either going to need to be completely rebuilt or replaced entirely. Either way would be expensive and still wouldn't get the truck back to Madison. Some family friends with an auto repair and towing business helped arrange the buying of a new engine wholesale and getting the remains of the truck brought back to Madison. They were even good enough to install it at their shop at cost.

All in all, it had all the hallmarks of a first road trip. Broke, stranded, unsuccessful in its ultimate goal, and with fallout that lasted months. Absolutely perfect.

BRANDED VII

A few helpful tips I've picked up along the way about having one's own custom temporary tattoos:

- It is usually, but not always, possible to use the condensation on the outside of a cold mixed drink to apply one.
- If done carefully they can be used as the equivalent of a wax seal on an envelope or postcard; the trick is to hold them under a dripping faucet and carefully watch the amount of water absorbed before dabbing with a napkin or washcloth. In the case of postcards, apply after writing. The underlying text remains visible.
- When applying to the window of a car, be sure to do so on the inside of the glass. Road grit will slowly wear away any tattoos applied to the outside.
- When applying to casual acquaintances, roughly one in one hundred people will become concerned that it is a way of ingesting drugs through the skin. Depending on their level of intoxication, reasoning with these individuals may not be possible.
- It's occasionally fun to apply one, discretely placed and consensually, to a partner postcoitus.

DILATANT COMPOUND

I can't claim that it was my idea originally. A friend at college had done an internship at a Bay Area tech company during the wackier periods of the first dot-com bubble, when it was important for each company to try being more eccentric than the last. He returned from his internship in the fall with a marvelous possession: five pounds of the chemical compound known popularly as Silly Putty. Many ceiling tiles were damaged in the aftermath; sometimes it can bounce amazingly.

Silly Putty is very definitely a trade name. Dow Chemical, inventor of the substance, calls it Dilatant Compound 3179 and continues to manufacture and sell it. Dow doesn't really deal with individuals, and their minimum purchase order at the time was $500.

Neither of which proved a problem for me a couple of years after college. Given the means, I couldn't imagine *not* ordering a hundred pounds of Silly Putty. There was no moment where I weighed the decision and considered it. It was simply obvious to me that it had to be done.

The general plan, having acquired all this material, would be to cut it into smaller quantities and resell it at a markup.

Standard business model, long since proven. Buy wholesale, sell retail.

My first hundred pounds got delivered on a nice spring day. Most people have only encountered this substance in quantities of less than one ounce. Two fifty-pound boxes are roughly the size of three twenty-four packs of soda. The stuff is **dense**. My unfortunate luck was that I lived in a townhouse and immediately had to carry it up a tall flight of stairs.

Then I had to divide it. And, as you may know, Silly Putty isn't prone to being divided.

Compound 3179 is resilient to say the least. The faster you come at it, the more it resists, unless some magic speed-and-angle combination occurs, when it just fractures. After several failed attempts to separate parts of it, I found the best implement was a cheap serrated steak knife. Slow slicing seemed to work, but it required a great deal of manual effort. I spent a lot of time on my patio, shirtless and wearing a surgical mask and gloves, slicing and weighing small pieces to make one- and five-pound bags. In retrospect I'm surprised no one called Homeland Security. It really couldn't have looked more suspicious.

Having worked out a method for cutting, bagging, and selling 3179, I settled into a nice ritual of bringing small bags of it to work and conventions. The markup was reasonable by the standards of toys, and tech workers in particular loved buying them. I sold fifty or sixty pounds at my work, then the rest of that batch at professional conferences. I invested in a second hundred pounds for further distribution. The money I made was never much, but it was a fun hobby.

While I was working my way through the second batch, I was invited to a corporate retreat in the San Juan Islands, in Puget Sound, not far from Seattle. There are ferries, but I was unwilling to spend a day driving and waiting for a boat. A small commuter airline had direct flights to Orcas Island Airport, a small, rural airport primarily used for private light planes and, rarely, commercial flights. The flight out of Seattle-Tacoma International Airport was uneventful. Compound 3179 doesn't read as anything dangerous on most airport security systems; it's not explosive or dense enough to be metal. At most, it got swabbed a couple of times, and the mass spectrometer cleared me of any malicious intent. Security at Sea-Tac didn't even blink.

The retreat was three days of battling corporate business units engaged in classic infighting and thankfully has no place in this narrative. Besides having a political pissing match with a VP and threatening to quit, it was comparatively unremarkable. It was good to leave.

Imagine Sunday afternoon at a tiny rural airport. No planes were on the ground yet, because they never stay longer than it takes to deplane and board the passengers. Even refueling is done at the other end, the round-trip distance to the island being well within the aircraft's safety margin. I was the first passenger to arrive. No X-ray machine, just a simple metal detector to walk through. The agent explained that she'd just need to hand-search my bag. *Sure,* I readily agreed. *Nothing to hide here.*

First thing out, my shaving kit. She unzipped it and found it uninteresting. Next, my laptop—nothing unusual there. My Palm Pilot. Extra batteries for my Nokia. And the myriad cables necessary for connecting all the above in a pre-Bluetooth age. Finally, the missing piece, a gallon freezer bag containing five pounds of a rubbery pink substance.

"Sir, can you explain this?" Thankfully the TSA hadn't started arming airport security at this point. The tone was pretty clear. If it happened today, I'd already be spread-eagled face down on the floor.

"It's just Silly Putty," I said, figuring this was a lot better than naming an obscure chemical compound, and trying to sound as calm and innocent as possible.

"Where on earth would you get that much Silly Putty?" Incredulity was better than hostility at this point.

"The Internet. It's way cheaper than buying those little eggs."

She sighed and looked me over. "Is Seattle your final destination today?" she asked.

"Yes, ma'am. I live in Issaquah. I'll be driving home from Sea-Tac."

"All right, I'm going to let you on this flight. But don't try to take this through another airport."

"Yes, ma'am, thank you. I won't." Polite, respectful, and not even a little bit true.

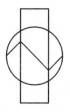

BRANDED VIII

Dear Mrs. Johnson,

I couldn't be happier with the finished stained glass piece! You captured the style and tone perfectly, and it looks fantastic catching the sunlight in my apartment.

Thank you again for taking on this commission. The pieces of yours that your son keeps in our office have always looked beautiful, and I'm very grateful that you were willing to attempt this for me.

Steven told me you were worried about the small cracks and bubbles in the glass, but I assure you it came out perfectly, and I wouldn't change a thing. Watching the different hues crawl across the floor has been amazing.

Thank you again with all my deepest gratitude . . .

TROUBLE

When I talked about her with friends, I always just called her Trouble. The nickname wasn't an exaggeration or hyperbole. I knew her during a period of my life when it seemed simpler to use code names for the girls I was seeing when describing them to my friends. I was having a lot of short, brutish, and nasty relationships. My friends couldn't be expected to keep track of a Tracie vs. a Tara, but they would remember "Birmingham" and "Proto-Trouble."

The first part of my second intermatrium was a time of deliberately poor choices. I stayed out too late and drank too much. I took rides home from strangers I'd met out clubbing. I was promiscuous even by my standards and was having unsafe sex more often than not. Trouble was the nadir.

She'd always been in trouble. I welcomed that. I wanted Trouble.

I met her via Craigslist, which probably dates this story fairly clearly. She came over and we started dating, to the extent that relatively casual sex can be considered dating. I'd meet up with her at the nightclub we both liked and hang out with her occasionally. She had great tattoos and a hard-luck story. I was working a swing shift, covering any potential problems that might happen with The Company's network, which made midnight my happy hour, and she apparently was a night person, so it was convenient to meet up afterward. We'd hang out for a while, and then I'd usually drive her to wherever she was staying that night. It seemed to vary; she was always crashing with different friends. Occasionally I'd drop her off at places she didn't refer to as a friend's home. That, and a few other signs, made it pretty clear that she was an escort. It didn't particularly bother me.

The first thing that did bother me was a conversation we had one night when I was driving her back to a friend's place on Capitol Hill. Somehow the conversation led to dangerous situations and dangerous friends.

"It's okay," I reassured her. "I've got a gun in the car, and my license is current."

"I can't be around guns," she said, her voice oddly flat.

While trying to navigate traffic, I looked over at her. "No, it's really okay; it's in the trunk, and it's all legal."

"No. It's a violation of my parole. I can't be around guns."

I had nothing to say. I hadn't known until then that she was on parole or had a criminal history. The last few blocks were quiet. I dropped her off, got my hug, and told her I'd get the locked box of unloaded firearms out of the trunk of the car. It had been the safest place to store them—until then.

The second worrisome moment was a week or so later. She was going to stay over at my apartment for the first time. I'd assumed she'd sleep in the bedroom with me, familiar territory for her, but she declined in favor of the couch.

"Do you have a blanket?"

"I think so. Are you sure you want to sleep on the couch?"

"It's just safest." An odd comment that I let slide.

When I'd gotten the spare blanket out of the closet, she explained a little more.

"I don't know where I am when I wake up, and maybe I'm back in prison or back—"

"Okay," I interjected. "Okay, stay on the couch. The cat stays close to me anyway."

She replied, "I'm sorry. I just don't want to cut you by accident." And from nowhere, three sliver-thin throwing knives appeared. Sharper and better than any knives I'd ever owned. I tucked her in and went to bed.

There were a couple of other warning signs as well. In conversation we discovered we had some acquaintances in common, all of whom, when I asked their advice, warned me to steer clear, due to her history of drugs and violence. Since these concerns came from people I considered friends and who pointedly did not consider her a friend, I took them fairly seriously. As Trouble and I spent more time together, she told me stories about a miscarriage earlier in the year, a difficult ex, and a restraining order.

By this point we'd been dating for all of three weeks, and I realized that I was in way over my head. There was more drama here than I was prepared to handle. I decided I had to stop seeing her. But breaking up with someone with a fairly serious history of violence is not to be done cavalierly.

The breakup went remarkably well, considering. I explained that the situation was too intense for me, something I didn't want in my life. This did not appear to be a huge shock to her; I think she realized how overwhelming it must be to someone she'd only started dating. We had a good talk about it and parted amicably. A couple of days later I got the following text:

> U made me remember how 2 smile and i finally got strong enough 2 leave him. I never meant 2 b such a mess. I really wanted 2 sleep next 2 u. I was just scared 2 trust again. If u ever change ur mind u know where 2 find me.

We did remain friends. She'd call or text me occasionally if she was in the neighborhood and come by the apartment. Usually I'd cook her something while we caught up and then give her a ride someplace. This went on sporadically for about five months, with a handful of visits or calls during that time.

I had long gotten past the compulsion to answer the phone in the middle of the night, doubly so for calls from blocked or unknown numbers. However, I had not yet learned to turn the ringer to silent at night, so I was awakened at 4:00 a.m. by an incoming call. Seeing the message *<blocked number>* on the display, I hit "End" and rolled over to return to sleep. This was short-lived, as the phone rang again immediately. On the assumption that they'd keep calling indefinitely at this point, I answered. A recorded voice informed me, "You are receiving a call from the King County Correctional System. The inmate *<name>* is attempting to call you. Press one to accept the call."

I took the call.

She wasn't making much sense, and it took a while for me to get the story straight. I won't even try to reproduce the conversation here. The narrative that took shape seemed to be that she was living in a weekly motel south of downtown. Her ex-boyfriend, who had a restraining order against her, had shown up at the motel, and they got into a fight. The motel called the cops, and despite the fact that he was in *her* room, she was arrested because she didn't leave the premises upon his arrival. Is that really how the law works? I'm not sure, but I thankfully have never had cause to know. Regardless of how she got there, she was in County and wanted a couple of favors. Surprisingly, being bailed out was not one of them. Her actual requests were more pragmatic and feasible; she wanted me to call the motel and have them box and store her things, using the credit she had for the room to cover the costs. She wanted me to lend her sixty dollars and drop it off at her storage unit so that they wouldn't seize her belongings in the interim. Lastly, she wanted me to track her on the county's Jail Inmate Lookup website to see what was happening. This required getting her full legal name and date of birth, neither of which I had known until then.

These seemed like reasonable requests. I called the motel right away, and the night clerk knew exactly who I was talking about and agreed to handle packing and storing her things. It was still possible to get a few hours' rest even with the detour to the storage unit before work, so I set an alarm and tried to sleep. It was not particularly restful. The next day I dropped off sixty dollars at the storage place before work, deliberately paying cash. I didn't want to leave any record.

A common myth about being arrested is that everyone gets one free phone call. In the King County jail you can make as many free phone calls as you want from the holding cell, as long as you accept the complete lack of privacy inherent in being on a speakerphone in front of the other inmates. It's not a pleasant experience. Once you have been processed out of holding and into a unit, as the modern cells are called, phone calls must be made collect or through a private telephone provider at exorbitant rates. In order to accept these calls, it is necessary to create an account with the provider and place money in it via a credit card.

It seemed worth it to put down some money in such an account to hear from her on occasion. I filled out the online form and paid twenty dollars with a credit card that had good fraud protection.

Trouble called again a few days later to check that I'd taken care of everything. I assured her that I had, and she had a couple of additional requests. She still had no desire to make bail, stating that she felt safer on the inside. What she did want from me were visits and pictures, neither of which I was enthusiastic about. I didn't really want a larger paper trail connecting me to someone who was regularly in serious trouble with the law.

And I was uncomfortable being dragged into a legal morass for someone whose surname I hadn't known a week ago. I demurred to both of these requests.

We wrapped up the call, and after she hung up, a computer-generated voice came on to report that we had spoken for eleven minutes, reducing my balance to fifty-four trillion, two hundred and forty-something billion, and assorted small change after that. This was obviously a surprise, as I did not recall depositing over three times the country's gross domestic product into a prison phone account. After a quick check with my credit card company's website showed that I had only paid twenty dollars, I suddenly saw the answer—the amount they'd credited to me was a truncated version of the credit card number I had used to pay. I'm not being glib; those really are the first digits of Citi MasterCard numbers. This either meant that the provider's software was truly, truly terrible or that the web submissions were then being manually entered into a system with no sanity checks whatsoever by someone not paying particular attention. Such is the privatization of correctional services. I didn't bother to contact them to resolve the issue, and as far as I know I still have a credit with them the size of the industrialized world's GDP.

She and I spoke occasionally over that summer—nothing of importance really, just small talk to break up the boredom of her confinement. She'd have minor updates on her case sometimes, figuring out if the boyfriend's restraining order itself had been falsely obtained, if he had perjured himself, if she could get out if he had. This went on for months. I never visited or sent pictures, but I kept taking the calls.

Around the end of the summer, she called to let me know she'd be getting released soon. I congratulated her and told her to give me a call when she got out, and we'd get dinner or something. She seemed enthusiastic, but it didn't come together. A month passed, then another. The last phone number she'd had before jail was disconnected, but she'd gone through phone numbers before, and I didn't think too much of it. Periodically I'd check the online inmate finder to see if she'd been incarcerated again; all it ever told me was that she'd been released.

I like to think that she got her life together, moved out of state, and is happy and healthy somewhere, but I know that's wishful thinking. She was already so far gone that her life wasn't going to change. There are a few people who can turn around after multiple felonies and substance abuse issues, but it's incredibly rare. Nothing about her made that look likely. I'm not sorry I knew her—it was an interesting view into that world—but I'm saddened by having seen up close how easily people can be written off by society.

BRANDED IX

A few years after the stained glass piece, my logo was given the most exposure I ever achieved. The local alternative newspaper runs a charity auction every fall, selling off goods donated by local businesses, novel events such as pizza and beer with the mayor, and some items of their own: movie night with their movie critic (winner's choice of movie), a full-page ad in one issue of the print edition, or all the advertising on their website for a full twenty-four hours. I bid on and won the last.

In my initial meeting with the paper's ad director, she was amused that I intended to run the same graphic in every one of the various ad sizes provided on the site. I think it was best regarded as some sort of conceptual art. We spent some time getting things arranged for the big day, and I registered a throwaway domain and hosted it on a friend's web server. Every visitor to the paper's website was shown one of six images of my logo at random, which would change on refresh. I installed an analytics package on the site to track visitors to my domain.

The ads launched at midnight, Pacific time. It was a full barrage; a full-height version of my logo split in half flanked either side, a narrow banner marked the top, and several medium-sized rectangles sat next to the news stories. Visitors started trickling in. The visits reached a temporary plateau by morning and then had a massive spike around lunchtime. The comment threads on unrelated articles became overrun with speculations about what had happened to the site. The most prevalent theory was that the site had somehow been hacked. By midafternoon the paper's blog had to run an article about the ads themselves, because the editorial staff had been getting e-mails wanting to know what happened. The journalist who wrote the post acknowledged that he'd also been confused until remembering it had been an auction item. The article included some quotes from outraged readers who were angry about the ads for various reasons, ranging from the aesthetic to the purely confused. The reporter, who left me anonymous, simply said, "A local guy" bought the auction item "because he wanted the world to see this design of his that has personal meaning to him. He's not trying to sell anything or get out any message," and followed up with another reminder that all the money I paid for it went to charity.

Then began the Rorschach test that was the comments thread. Most of the comments ranged from "modified yin yang," to rip-offs of various band logos, to an AC circuit design, to some sort of neofascist emblem, and finally to a new street sign logo prohibiting driving through a tunnel. There were more comments arguing that the design was just ugly, that I had overpaid—for charity—for the opportunity, as well as compliments. Some said it was less intrusive than the fairly risqué ads for adult toys that normally ran in some of the ad spaces. Finally some of my friends enjoyed trolling the other commenters. My favorite of my friends' comments claimed it was a Magic Eye poster.

When all was said and done, over three hundred thousand unique individuals had viewed my ad. Of those, around one in a hundred clicked through to see the random image site. The ad director for the paper informed me that was roughly double the normal rate they expected for any ad. Obviously some of that was the lure of novelty combined with the mystery of being ubiquitous on the site. According to the data I logged, the average visitor to my site stayed on it for slightly over a minute and hit refresh twice during that time, presumably in the hopes that it had simply incorrectly loaded the first time, then quit in annoyance. I consider the entire experience well worth the money.

KNIFED

In 1992, James Madison Memorial High School had a school shooting. In the pre-Columbine age a shooting in the parking lot of a suburban high school was still shocking. It bore little resemblance to the modern definition of a school shooting, and it was, in fact, a drug deal gone bad between truant students in the parking lot. However, Madison's schools had no history of that level of violence, and as a response, the school board passed a zero tolerance policy on weapons in schools.

Zero tolerance policies are almost always a bad idea, and this was not an exception.

Two years later, in my final year of high school, I had already been accepted to a university, and it was obvious that I was going to graduate with more than enough credits. As a senior I was allowed to leave early any day I didn't have a class during the last period. It was a perk I declined, working instead as a volunteer tutor for younger students. This wasn't entirely altruistic; I was sleeping with one of them. Her mother knew what was happening but was glad to stop getting truancy calls and at least reassured to know her daughter was finishing her homework and getting better grades.

Still, she was just one of the students I was tutoring; the rest of them I *had* taken on for more or less altruistic reasons.

So, one perfectly normal Thursday afternoon, I was in the tutoring center, teaching algebra to a freshman, when my pen broke. It was just a crappy disposable pen, the kind that can usually be fixed by opening it and blowing into the ink tube to add a little pressure. With fingernails too short to pry the plastic pieces apart, I produced the trusty Swiss Army knife that I'd had since the age of ten. I had just begun repairs with the flathead screwdriver when one of the vice-principals entered.

"What do you have there, Gus?"

This seemed like a trap. I chose to avoid the question. "A screwdriver?"

"No, the whole thing. What is that?"

"A tool?"

He was having none of it. "That's a knife. Give it to me, and I'm afraid you're going to need to come down to the head office." And down we went.

The faculty and administration of the school, apart from him, were generally inclined to give me the benefit of the doubt. My first stepfather had been a vice-principal there my freshman year but had since moved on.

The vice-principal laid out the facts as he saw them. Sadly, under the zero tolerance policy, I was, in fact, in violation of school district rules. I blamed this mostly on the district's overly broad definition of *weapon*. The principal was sympathetic toward me. A few years earlier she'd calculated every possibility and decided that generally being lenient toward me about small things was safer and easier than dealing with me being truculent. I believe that she knew I was the one running the satirical underground newspaper, for example, but thought it was harmless enough to leave alone. This time she had no power to prevent an expulsion hearing. She did use her limited authority to cancel my suspension prior to the hearing and recommended that I be allowed to remain in school, but beyond that her hands were tied, and the decision on expulsion would be made at the district level.

Some members of the faculty were incredibly supportive. My Advanced Placement Chemistry teacher, an excellent educator nearing retirement, brandished his pocketknife in the air in class and yelled, "What'll they make me do, retire?" He was one of several teachers who wrote letters to the school district recommending I not be expelled.

My hearing was held the week after the initial incident. My twenty-year-old sister accompanied me as my nominal but unofficial guardian. My mother had departed earlier that year to pursue the man who would eventually be her third husband. No one seemed to find it odd that my adult representative was my older sister, herself in the gray area between eighteen and twenty-one, where one is legally neither an adult nor a minor.

The hearing was held at the school district's central office downtown, a disused former elementary school that had been converted to offices when the neighborhood started to be dominated by university students without kids. The assistant superintendent for the south and west districts was presiding over my hearing.

"So, young man, it seems like you've gotten into some unusual trouble for a student like you."

"I guess."

"You were caught with a weapon on school grounds. That's pretty serious. What do you have to say for yourself?"

"It's not a weapon. It's a pocketknife."

"Well, it has a sharp blade, so under district policy it's a knife."

I'd brought some letters of support with me, and I offered them to him.

"Here are two letters from my teachers, one from my principal, and one from my scoutmaster."

"Well, in light of your lack of prior offenses and your outstanding academic record, I'm prepared to admit you back into the student body."

I sat impassive, dissociated. My lack of reaction seemed to spook him, and he spoke again hastily.

"There won't be any mark on your permanent record about any of this."

I left.

·

Three months later, every National Merit Scholar from the district was invited to appear at a school board meeting to be congratulated. One student from each of the four high schools was invited to give a short speech. Aside from the four speakers, the rest of us were just there to do a handshake line with the school board so they could make bland congratulatory statements to us while being filmed for local public access television. I was not the one selected by my school to speak, and my friend Trevor's attempt to cede time to me was not successful.

My father and fair-weather stepmother were thrilled to attend, completely unaware of what had transpired and my loathing for the school board.

My place in line was about third back from the beginning. When I got to the first board member, instead of letting go of his hand after he said congratulations, I kept my grip firm, made eye contact, and asked, "Can you explain to me why a nonlocking pocketknife is considered a weapon under district policy?" His eyebrows went up, as he was not expecting questions from the props.

"Well, you see, it could still potentially be used against another student or a teacher as a weapon—"

"That is a stupid argument," I said, cutting him off, still holding his hand firmly. "You hand out compasses in geometry class that are basically ice picks. Home Ec is full of knives. I've had a Swiss Army knife since I was ten."

The next board member was growing concerned that I hadn't just accepted my glad-handing and moved along. The students in line behind me were getting impatient. Neither of these things concerned me. I didn't let go of his hand.

"Well, possibly the policy is overly broad—"

I stopped him again.

"Three months ago you tried to expel me, and now you're trotting me out as a successful product of this district. You can't have it both ways."

"Well, we obviously didn't expel you, because you're here." Not a bad rejoinder, even if kind of a self-righteous one.

"Yeah, and the local private high schools wouldn't have minded padding their stats with someone with my test scores. Don't pretend you did me any favors."

By this point, since I was still firmly holding his right hand, three students had accepted an awkward left-handed handshake from this member of the school board.

"Well, I'm sorry you had a bad experience, but we're trying to make sure that all our students are safe in schools."

"You're doing a shitty job. I will vote against you next year when I'm an adult." I let his hand go and proceeded to the next board member.

Repeat that conversation six more times. I was the last student to leave the stage, and I told each and every school board member what I thought of the pointlessness of zero tolerance. None of them had any better retort than the first poor board member, and none of them had really thought the issue through at any real level. *No weapons* was the kind of no-brainer vote that they all wanted to be on record as having supported. Embarrassing them in their televised little pageant was delicious, although I did have to provide my father and stepmother with a bit of explanation as to why I was on the stage so long.

I didn't stop carrying my pocketknife, and I graduated with honors four months later.

Never forgive, never forget. Revenge is a dish best served cold. Pick your angry cliché.

BRANDED X

The next idea was the first to embed the logo inside another design. At the time, I was driving an older BMW, not old enough to be classic, but old enough that I wouldn't mind making some custom changes. Which I did. The end result was a circular design the same size as the BMW roundel, with the logo in the middle on a white field, a thick black ring around it and the initials of my *nom de internet* arranged in the same arc as the BMW letters. Finding an online print shop was trivial. I uploaded my artwork and had a batch of stickers printed, far more than I needed to customize the car, and found stores online that would sell replacements for the original roundels in case I was disappointed with the results.

I never got around to actually decorating the car. The spare roundels were completed but never installed. The stickers by themselves have gone on to be popular in their own right and have ended up stuck in unlikely places in half a dozen countries. I'm fairly sure the statute of limitations is up for vandalizing an obstinate ATM in Belgium with one.

TELEPHONE

"Hello?"

Laughter on the other end of the line. "Hey, is this 4-DICK?" followed by more laughter.

I stood transfixed, looking at the touch-tone pad on the phone, matching up the numbers to letters. Sure enough, the last four digits of my new phone number—3-4-2-5—do indeed spell *dick*, among other things.

"Yes," I said, calmly but befuddled, still staring at the letters on the buttons. "Yes, it is." I hung up the phone.

The phones in the dormitories were part of the university phone system, which only required dialing five digits for other internal numbers. For technical reasons I cannot fathom, this also meant that numbers were statically assigned to rooms. My roommate and I had unwittingly ended up with this number when we'd requested a better room than we'd had our freshman year. The first call came at the very beginning of the semester, and the calls came throughout the year, primarily on weekends, when the student body was drunker than usual.

Unfortunately for the callers, Jason and I had sharp wits and no shame.

"Hello?"

"Hi, is this 4-DICK?"

"It is! Is this takeout or delivery?"

"What?"

"You called for dick. Would you like it for takeout or delivery?"

They'd usually hang up at that point. Depending on how misanthropic we were feeling, sometimes we'd use the recall function commonly known as *69 to call them back.

"Hello?"

"Sorry, sir, we seem to have gotten disconnected. We were discussing your dick order?"

"What? Fuck you."

"You called us. The number is quite clear that it's for dick."

This was another prime bailout point, but depending on some combination of intoxication and belligerence, sometimes our caller would continue.

"Faggot!"

"Sir, I'm just the receptionist, and my sexual orientation isn't relevant here. Do you want dick or not? We don't judge."

Pretty much no one got past there. On the rare occasions that they did, we'd just improvise in the same vein. Oddly no one ever left messages on our answering machine. Prank calls are apparently less fun if a human doesn't answer.

The number of calls dropped precipitously after a couple of months. My personal suspicion is that there is a limited number of people who find making prank calls entertaining, and once we'd made it clear that we weren't going to feel ashamed or bothered about being 4-DICK, they had no further reason to bother us.

BRANDED XI

I was still dissatisfied with the lack of utility that any of my prior product attempts provided to the people receiving them. Temporary tattoos are ephemeral. The cards are only used once. Stickers are decorative but of limited usefulness. I wanted something people could use repeatedly, something they would *want* to use that just happened to have my logo on it.

Once again, the impetus for a new idea came from something I saw by chance. While on a trip to Las Vegas, I realized most of the casinos had their own custom playing cards, ostensibly to prevent would-be cheaters from sneaking in their own aces.

Playing cards are fun. Every household has at least one deck, and souvenir decks are a staple of gift shops. Being able to produce a pack of cards during dull moments is very useful. Even just being able to play solitaire is a substantial improvement to being bored; serious backpacking guidebooks recommend taking along a deck of cards, as the value of entertainment far outweighs the negligible extra burden. People like having cards around. My decision was made.

The Internet again made this surprisingly easy. There were only a few questions: Large or small cards, laminated paper or all plastic, back design only or customized fronts? Because some of these choices forced a larger minimum order—even I found buying a thousand decks of cards ridiculous—the choices were remarkably simple. I opted for custom backs but standard numerals and imagery. Plastic cards had a much larger minimum order, leaving me to pick laminated paper. Paper boxes were an extra that I decided were worth the cost. Shipping was mildly delayed due to an inconvenient hurricane, but before long I had enough decks of cards to run a small casino.

BILLINGS

Between my junior and senior years of college I moved to Seattle for the summer to see if it was really a place I wanted to live after graduation and if my long-distance girlfriend and I could actually make it work if we saw each other more than twice a semester. As soon as finals ended, I threw nearly everything I owned into a rental truck and drove west on Interstate 90 until it ended on the Seattle waterfront.

I found a sublet with a friend of my girlfriend. That summer was a blur of temp jobs and dates. The tech industry was ravenous for more people, particularly those willing to work without any hope of benefits or long-term guarantees of further employment. I found a temp agency I liked that assigned me a decent handler and found me several positions over the summer, some much better than others. The final one in particular was problematic and often neglected to pay the temp agency.

My handler at the temp agency assured me that it would all get worked out, but it was hard not to notice that they still weren't paying *me* until *they* got paid. This came at a pretty bad time. Summer was ending, and I needed cash to rent the truck to move back and cover gas and motels on the way home.

Direct deposit wasn't really available yet. I'd been sending paychecks back to my credit union in Wisconsin by first-class mail, but it took up to a week for the funds to actually appear. I'd reserved the truck using the last of my credit card limit, but I didn't have enough to cover two thousand miles' worth of gasoline, even if I slept in the truck to save on motels. I needed cash, especially for some of the smaller communities that still weren't fond of taking out-of-state checks.

My last regular paycheck had been dropped in the mail to the credit union the Friday before I planned on leaving, and I was checking online banking every day to see if it had cleared. My second-to-last paycheck became available on the day I'd initially planned to depart. I was able to sign it over to my girlfriend to get some ready cash, but her bank didn't really trust her due to poor credit and wouldn't advance the full amount. Two days later, on my drop-dead moving date, my handler let me know that I could pick up my last paycheck at their office in the eastern suburbs. I drove by in my rental truck and picked it up on my way out of town. It was the Friday of the long Labor Day holiday weekend.

An important segue: student housing at the University of Wisconsin in the nineties was a viciously competitive market. All the leases in student neighborhoods end on August 14 and start on August 15, leaving everyone homeless for one night. Good apartments were rented as early as January, with an August 15 move-in date. After we'd each had suboptimal living situations the previous year, my best friend Matt and I had gotten organized in February and found a great unit in a triplex just off campus. Finding it had been a lengthy process involving abusing my access to GIS software at my job, a six-pack of SURGE, the university-approved landlord list, and hours of midnineties industrial music.

The upshot of all that was that we'd already had a great apartment for two weeks, and that I hadn't seen it except for a brief tour six months prior. Fortunately Matt had emailed me the address and the new phone number he'd arranged before I left Seattle.

The first day's drive was okay. Since I'd had checks printed with my Washington address, the gas station in Spokane was willing to take a check, as was the motel. Spokane does grudgingly admit Seattle is in the same state, for financial if not political or social issues. I checked in with my girlfriend and Matt on the phone. Matt had set our new answering machine message to "House of Matt and Gus! Leave a message!"

By early Saturday morning I had crossed into Montana. The last thing resembling a city on I-90 before Minneapolis is Billings. Hoping to cash my last check, I got off the interstate and started looking for a check-cashing or payday loan joint. Have you ever noticed how they're always in the worst neighborhoods?

The cashier was fairly pleasant, despite being behind bulletproof glass. She asked for ID, of which I had plenty, and also had a few questions about my residence. She then vanished into the back with my check, my documents, and the form I'd completed. I sat patiently in the waiting room. Sometimes you just have to wait.

She reemerged after a bit, smiled pleasantly, and doled out the cash for my check, less their 2 percent commission for payroll checks. Twenty, forty, sixty, eighty, one hundred, twenty, forty, sixty, eighty, one hundred eighty-seven. She smiled and wished me the best. I drove away.

My next stop was in Rapid City, South Dakota, five hours away. I stopped to get gas and check back in with my girlfriend in Seattle and Matt in Madison. I was a long-haired goth kid wearing a biker jacket and driving a rental truck who'd stopped to use a pay phone. Honestly, if I had been a small town cop, I'd have suspected me. The call to my girlfriend got her voice mail. Nothing unexpected. When I called the landline at Matt's and my new place, I got this message: *Hi, you've reached the House of Matt and Gus! If this is Gus, please page me right away.*

I paged Matt from the gas station. If I had looked sketchy making a call from the pay phone, it had to have been much worse hanging around one of the last pay phones in the country that took incoming calls. It was a few minutes before he called, and I think the teenage girl behind the counter wanted to leave with me; I was obviously going somewhere better.

The pay phone rang, and I answered. "Hello?"

Matt on the other end of the line: "What the hell happened?"

Completely dumbfounded, I asked, "What?"

"Did you get arrested?"

"What? No!"

"Then what the hell was that call about?"

"What do you mean?"

Matt proceeded to explain that he'd gotten a call from a woman who wanted to confirm my physical appearance, residence, and last known whereabouts. After a series of pleasant questions, she thanked him and was about to disconnect. He interrupted.

"Hey, what's all this about?"

Her answer remains priceless. "Oh," she said, "I'm just helping Gus get out of Montana," and she hung up.

BRANDED XII

The next idea was shamelessly stolen from a package I received from an electronics vendor. To prevent, or at least detect, tampering with the package in transit, they had used a uniquely patterned tape. The theory was that, should a thief steal the expensive computer parts, they would be unable to cover their tracks due to their not having the proprietary tape to reseal the package. It also served as a nice reminder of their brand for the consumer, who would have to look at the repeated logo while slicing open the package.

Branded tape proved to be surprisingly easy. Ordering office and shipping supplies over the Internet had become the norm, not the exception. Again, the variety of options was limited only by the amount of money I wanted to throw at the project. Clear or opaque? Color graphic or black outline? Length of the roll? Width of tape? Thickness of tape? The possibilities seemed endless.

In the end I chose transparent tape with the logo's black lines on a two-inch-wide roll. The mailroom in my building was demonstrably concerned when a pair of very heavy yet small boxes was delivered; the concierge debated asking me what they were but decided he didn't want to know.

The design came out perfectly, although I do regret going with the slightly thinner tape. It gives it a little bit of a cheap feeling and is prone to the problem thinner tapes have of splitting when pulled unevenly.

COLD WHITE TILES

This was how our normal Tuesdays would go. She'd text:

> Hey im working want to get a drink at nn when I
> go on break?

I'd answer:

> Yeah sounds good let me know when and I'll
> head down.

It had become our pattern. Seattle strip clubs can't serve alcohol, something neither the patrons, nor the staff, nor the owners prefer. I was in the first category; she was in the second. It was another one of those Tuesday nights.

> I'm drinking b4 work. U want to meet up at the
> usual early?

> Sorry can't. out at a dinner with friends. Free
> later.

K txt when your ready ill go on break

K probably at like 8:30. I'll be at the bar come
over when you can

I arrived at the bar first and got a booth. She arrived not
long after with a friend in tow. They joined me, and I ordered
us a round of drinks. Light conversation and a second round
of drinks were had before they decided to head back to work.
To keep them out of trouble at the club, which has pretty strict
rules about fraternization with customers, I waited at the bar
for another drink to give them time to get back and changed
into work clothes.

After finishing my drink I walked over to the club, paid my
cover, and found a seat not too close to the stage. Sitting at the
rail implies tipping, usually with an active interest in seeing the
dancer for a private dance after the stage shift. Sitting a row or
two back sends a different message. I enjoyed the stage show
for a bit, politely declined a couple of offers of private shows
with the correct response of "No thank you, I'm waiting for
someone." Most strippers prioritize not poaching each other's
regulars, as well as not having their time wasted on a customer
who isn't going to spend.

She came out on the floor and found me, sat down in my
lap, and put her arm around my neck. "Come on, let's go get
a booth in back," she said and pulled me out of the chair. On
slow nights the back of the club was mostly empty except for
the booths used for private dances. We settled into one and
waited for the next song to start. She was sitting next to me,
resting her head on my shoulder. When the song ended, she
sat up and shook her head. "Give me a minute. I'm going to run
to the restroom. Can you watch my purse and shoes?" I readily agreed. "Okay, I'll be quick. I'm going to cheat and use the

men's room back here instead of going all the way to the locker room." She kissed my cheek and got up.

A song passed, then two. If she hadn't left her stuff with me, I'd have felt ditched. After the third song I decided I had to go check on her. Taking her belongings with me, I headed for the restroom.

The transition from a dimly lit club floor to a brightly lit white-tiled bathroom is always jarring. This transition was worse than most; she was sitting on the floor underneath the paper towel dispenser with her eyes closed. When I shook her by the shoulder, she half opened her eyes and asked me to sit down with her. I acquiesced and sat next to her, putting her shoes and purse on the floor.

"Hey," I said. "Hey, stay awake, okay? We need to get up. Can you stand up?" She clutched my arm and half mumbled something barely audibly. "What is it, sweetheart? Can you say it again?"

She mumbled again. I made out some of her words: "Please stay here. I'm tired."

"Okay, okay. I'm here." She rested her head on my shoulder. We sat quietly on the floor for a while.

The door opened, and another one of the dancers came into the room. She glared at me as she took in the scene. "What the hell are you doing?" she asked angrily. "Who are you? What'd you do to her?"

I stood up and kept my hands visible. "I didn't do anything to her. She asked me to sit with her. All her stuff's right there. I'm just gonna leave, okay?"

"Get out."

I complied, giving her broad latitude on my way out of the bathroom. Once I was on the club floor, I hurried to the door and left. It was a confusing walk home.

From: <redacted>@gmail.com
To: me
Subject: Oh lord
Date: March 4, <redacted>

I am so sorry for the train wreck that was me last night.
And brandi feels really bad for snapping at you, she
didn't know who you were and seeing me passed out on
a strange man made her nervous. Thank you so much
for taking care of me . . . I had a great time til I made the
ill decision to smoke weed. Hope you're not too trauma-
tized by the experience.
x

Sent via BlackBerry from T-Mobile

It'd be cliché to say that nothing was the same after that or that I didn't see her again. That wasn't the case. Things went back to normal for a few months, including grabbing drinks outside of her work. We fell back into our pattern, that one bad experience vanishing like a ripple in smooth water.

When she told me she was going to move away from Seattle, it wasn't a surprise, and it was the right choice for her. Still, that one moment defined my relationship with her, and it's all that stands out when I think of her: being afraid of being blamed and punished for trying to do the right thing.

BRANDED XIII

For about a decade I'd had an old flat-panel monitor lying around, a leftover from a previous job and no longer particularly useful. The display was a nineteen-inch LCD mounted on a wildly overbuilt pedestal, the manufacturer apparently having left a large area for some potential future expansion that never materialized. The maximum resolution was fairly pathetic by modern standards, so I had just let it collect dust, waiting for an idea of how it could be useful.

The answer came as part of the nascent "maker" movement, a do-it-yourself hobbyist culture driven by increasingly affordable small electronics and an interest in building devices that utilized them to do novel things. One of the better offerings was the Raspberry Pi, a credit card–sized computer designed to help teach children programming. At thirty-five dollars it had rapidly become a favorite for hobbyists, due particularly to the numerous expansion ports it offered. Other similar devices followed and ended up being used in ways their designers never anticipated.

With the help of a good friend who has a serious penchant for making things and a workshop to match, we built a sufficient bracket into the pedestal of the display to contain the

Raspberry Pi, including connecting it to the display, wiring up additional ports so they could be used externally, and stealing power from the display's power supply. I then configured the software to immediately display a full-sized picture of my logo and perform various visual effects on it, similar to popular screensaver patterns. In sum, I had a nineteen-inch display panel that requires a single power outlet, is easily portable, and does nothing but display my logo in various permutations. I refer to it as my "propaganda kiosk." It currently sits on the entryway table in my apartment to greet visitors.

KAMPFBEREIT

It was a Wednesday, near midnight, when the phone rang. The display read TARA CALLING, a not unusual late-night occurrence. I answered.

"Hello?"

"Gus, I need your help!"

"What's going on?"

"It's too long to explain on the phone, but I'm afraid they're watching the house. The doorbell keeps ringing, but I'm not answering. Can you come over?"

"Sure. How about I come get you, and we can go someplace and get dinner, okay?"

"Okay, just please hurry?"

It's difficult to describe our relationship in any standard terms. We weren't dating or hooking up, but we had a mutual trust that ran pretty deep. I'd gotten bad people out of her life, and she'd gotten bad thoughts out of mine. We took care of one another.

While I grabbed my car keys and my field jacket, I thought about what kind of trouble she was in now. She was twenty and made a lot of pretty bad choices. Many of her friends were people even I would class as undesirable. Not because they were petty criminals, but because they were *stupid* petty criminals. This was probably another dispute over stolen electronics or some minuscule amount of money or drugs. She tended to get caught in the middle of these things.

Once, one of her roommates had claimed to have hidden some meth in the house and then threatened to call the cops if she didn't pay him five hundred dollars. Since only her name was on the lease, he figured she'd take the fall. I chased him off, rekeyed the locks, and generally settled the situation. He never came back.

With stories like that one playing in my mind, I hesitated to leave my apartment. I sat down at the desk and reached underneath to where the safe was mounted and keyed in the combination. The spring-loaded door snapped open, and I withdrew my pistol. The full magazine was next to it. I checked the spring and slipped the magazine into the body of the gun. I racked the slide once, hearing the menacing sound of the action, and it was ready to fire. I put it in its holster and slid it into my pocket.

During the drive over I thought about what to expect. The roads were empty. Seattle goes to sleep early. The house Tara rented on the back of Magnolia Hill was in a quiet residential neighborhood. The autumn night was dead still as I took the shortcut path through the neighbor's yard. There was never parking in the alley her house faced, and tonight I felt it best not to announce my destination to observers.

The porch light was off. I could see some second-story lights inside. Remembering her words about the doorbell, I called her cell phone instead of ringing the bell.

"Hello?"

"I'm on your porch. I don't see anybody else out here or in the alley. Wanna let me in?"

I could hear her steps on the stairs as she came down to the door. She looked frazzled when she opened the door but pretty in her dishevelment. Once the door was safely bolted behind me, she gave me a hug, seemingly more for her own sake than for mine.

"Thanks for coming over. I don't know what to do."

"It's okay. I was up anyway. You know I don't sleep." I didn't want to ask what was frightening her or what had happened. "Are you ready to go?"

"No, I want to change and wash my face. It'll only take a minute."

"Sure. Take your time."

We climbed the stairs to the second floor where the main living area was. Tara went into her bedroom and shut the door. I paced, out of boredom rather than anxiety. I looked out the window that faced the alley. I couldn't see anyone; the night looked completely still. I turned when I heard her bedroom door open again.

"Ready?" she asked. She looked a lot calmer than she had a few minutes earlier.

"Sure. I'm parked a street over. We can cut through the yard. Where do you want to eat?"

She named her favorite late-night restaurant. It wasn't a particular favorite of mine, but I had nothing against it and agreed. We descended the stairs to the door again, me leading. I stepped onto the porch and looked around, then gestured for her to follow. She locked the door, and we walked in darkness through the yard. My right hand was in my jacket pocket on the grip of the gun. My left hand found my car keys and was holding the alarm fob, thumb ready on the "Disarm" button.

The front lawn was moonlit as we stepped out of the shadows. The night was clear, with a slight hint of the colder weather to come. On the residential street the silence was incredible; there were no sounds except for our footsteps on the occasional fallen leaves.

The double beep of my car alarm disarming seemed deafening in the silence. We'd reached the car, and I opened her door for her. As she slid into her seat, I heard an engine start behind me, perhaps a block or so away. I slammed her door and looked behind me. I hadn't heard any other doors close. Someone was in their car watching us. I crossed to my side, opened the door, and ducked my head inside.

"Just stay in the car, okay?" I told her.

The black SUV had been facing the wrong way, assuming we'd be in the alley, and was too large to easily make a U-turn on the narrow neighborhood street. When they pulled up next to us, I had the bulk of the door between me and them.

There were at least two of them in the SUV. The rear windows were tinted, and I couldn't see in back. The passenger riding shotgun rolled the window down and looked menacingly at me.

"Who're you?"

In my pocket I felt my hand on the textured grip of the pistol. I placed my finger on the trigger and got ready to bring up the gun. "It doesn't matter who I am."

"We wanna talk with her."

"That's not going to happen right now." I tried to sound as resolute as possible.

We stared at each other in silence for what seemed like minutes. Finally he blinked, and they drove away. I took my hand off the gun, which was still securely in my pocket. Climbing into the driver's seat, I slammed my door and started the engine. Watching their taillights, I made a sharp U-turn and drove the other direction with my lights off for a few blocks. When I felt sure they hadn't tried to follow us, I switched on the lights and headed for our destination.

To this day I don't think she knows that I had a gun or that I was ready to use it.

BRANDED XIV

Rare in the pantheon of my branded merchandise, the lapel pins were neither my idea, nor did I design or implement them. They were a surprise gift from a girlfriend who clearly knew what I wanted.

It had become a bit of a tradition for me to throw an after-party for my work friends following our company's holiday party. The party was always large and held in venues sizable enough to hold a few thousand guests. The after-party was a much more intimate affair, from a dozen attendees the first year to double that five years later.

At this particular party, we were just getting started when I needed to run next door for additional supplies. While I was gone, my girlfriend dispensed a pin to every attendee to don immediately. They were all instructed not to say anything about the pins and to wait until I noticed.

Somewhat to her disappointment and despite my intoxication, it took me mere minutes to notice. Upon my realization, the whole story was told, and the remaining large bag of pins was produced. Humans are excellent at pattern recognition, and after two decades of placing my logo I can recognize it immediately. It was an excellent gift and remains one of the most popular items in the collection. It's discreet, easily applied and removed, and can be placed once on a jacket or bag without having to worry about moving it.

RED LIGHTS, BLUE TARP

The big doorman at the dive bar on the edge of the French Quarter had been giving us his best carnival barker attempt every time we'd gone past over the last several days. Given that we had to walk past the bar on the way from the hotel into the Quarter, this was rather frequent. Despite his attempts to persuade us, we were not particularly tempted. We were wary of anything too far from the safe-ish tourist places in the French Quarter, and this bar had no charm whatsoever. It looked run down even by the standards of pre-Katrina New Orleans.

However, we did end up there at the tail end of a night full of very poor decisions. It was a worse decision than we'd already made that week.

Matt and I had only ventured back out of the hotel in search of Gatorade or similar electrolyte-replenishing beverages after a long night of drinking and mishaps. Finding an open establishment that wasn't a bar in that part of town at 4:00 a.m. was tricky. Ultimately we failed and headed back to the hotel. Our route took us right past the aforementioned dive.

"Hey, you boys want to see some pretty ladies?" a gravelly voice that was almost a growl said. "C'mon, you've been walking past all week."

I don't really remember why this seemed like a good idea at the time, but it did. We entered. There was no cover.

The space was poorly lit even for a dive. It was less of a strip club than a bar that had some disaffected dancers just doing some drinking. There was an empty stage behind the bar. No DJ, only a jukebox. We approached the bar and took two of the many empty stools.

"What're you boys drinking?"

Matt answered. "Two vodka and tonics, please."

"We're outta vodka."

"Gin and tonics?"

"We're outta gin."

"What clear liquors do you have?"

"We've got Diesel."

For the uninitiated, Diesel is a neutral grain spirit that is roughly 90–95 percent alcohol, vaguely comparable to Everclear. Its main purposes are sterilizing equipment, cleaning jewelry, and maintaining late-stage alcoholism.

"Two Diesel and tonics then, please."

The bartender poured the drinks and placed them in front of us. While we were taking experimental, tiny sips to gauge the potency, he moved down the bar to rouse one of the strippers to get on stage. She took a couple of singles out of her purse to play the jukebox and put on some music. Heading behind the bar, she climbed up on the stage and began indifferently dancing. Swaying, really. Less sexy movement than simply dull motion. After two songs, she stopped and returned to her barstool for more of her drink. After a few gulps, she approached us.

"You boys looking for some fun? Want to get some champagne?"

I was morbidly tempted. "How much would that be?"

"Two hundred for the hour. Plus we get champagne."

I took it. She lead me farther back, into the recesses of the club.

The room was painted entirely black and had a single red lightbulb in a ceiling fixture. There was a chair in the middle of the room, the same sort one finds in lower-grade restaurants and banquet halls. There was no door, but once we were inside I saw a blue tarp hanging by one corner from a hook on one side of the doorway. She found another corner and put it on another hook on the other side of the doorway. The blue tarp under the red light looked almost as black as the walls. I sat down in the chair and she sat in my lap.

"Just wait a minute, honey. He'll be back with the champagne." This came to pass shortly, as the bartender brought two splits of champagne on a bar tray and handed them to us. There were no glasses. I passed on mine, not liking it being opened already. She didn't touch hers either, taking a small bottle of peach schnapps out of her purse. She took a pull on it and made an offering gesture toward me. I declined politely.

She asked my name, and I casually lied, telling her, "Alex." She found this somehow funny, laughed, and told me her name was Alexis, adding that it was just her work name. This appeared to amuse her tremendously.

"You have a dollar bill, honey?"

"I think so. Why?"

"There's a condom machine in the ladies' room."

This gave me some pause. "Huh?"

"You ever cheated on your wife before?"

"No."

A lot of times in life I just accept things that are happening as inevitable. I gave her the dollar, and she got up and left, pulling the tarp aside without unhooking it.

She probably wasn't gone long, but it seemed like forever. It didn't occur to me to leave or object. I'd now gone far enough that I couldn't see not following through. I sat in the poorly lit room and listened to the overhead music, some bland mix of songs off the jukebox that was the replacement for a club DJ.

When she got back we had mediocre sex. She straddled me while I was seated in the chair. I have very little memory of it; it simply wasn't interesting enough to remember. Afterward we talked for a bit. She had a sad story about how she ended up in New Orleans after losing her husband in a car wreck. I think I told her something of my sad story of the previous year. After a while she said it was time to go, and she took down the tarp, and we headed back out to the bar.

Matt was waiting, our two drinks untouched. "You okay?" he asked.

"Yeah, let's just get out of here."

We headed toward the entrance, where the doorman was still working. He turned to face us, his considerable bulk blocking the doorway entirely. "You boys got something for the doorman?" It wasn't really a question. We obviously weren't getting past him. I gave him ten bucks, and he let us leave.

It was nearly dawn, and the sky was starting to light up. We walked the two blocks back to the hotel in silence.

BRANDED XV

Early in our relationship, a girlfriend made me a wax seal. She'd previously been into a lot of crafting and wanted to give me a unique present. During a weekend when I was out of town, she made and discarded more than one prototype, eventually mastering her technique with the wood-burning tool to etch the outline of my logo into the flat end of a section of wooden dowel.

The presentation was lovely; she gave it to me in a small, beautiful wooden hinged box also containing four sticks of sealing wax. A particular type of wax is used for seals; it burns at a higher temperature than candle wax and hence can be melted to take an imprint.

I rarely used it, even before that relationship came to an ugly end. The wood is a bit too porous and the wax gets stuck in the grooves. After every use it requires a tedious cleaning process of scraping out the extra wax. The end result is that it can really only be used once per session, and as such only very significant documents receive a wax seal.

It was still a thoughtful idea. They can't all be winners.

MISTRESS

I should probably start by saying Francesca wasn't actually my mistress, at least in any sense of the word as it is commonly used. She was neither my partner in an extramarital affair, nor was she involved in any sort of power-play relationship. Regardless, I called her my mistress, and unlike most of the times I have assigned nicknames, she was both involved in the selection process and willing to refer to herself in that fashion when the circumstances warranted it.

Due to The Company's uncharacteristic slowness in updating the list of preferred hotels in New York City after our office moved, the only hotels I could get at the corporate discount rate were around Times Square rather than the new office location in Chelsea. I ended up staying a few blocks from Times Square, almost all the way to Eighth Avenue. During the nineties, the once-legendary seediness of Times Square was chased out of such a prime tourist destination by an ambitious mayor, but seediness cannot truly be destroyed. Hence Eighth Avenue at the time of my visit.

Even on my first work trip to NYC I already had some coworkers-cum-drinking buddies-cum-friends thanks to the magic of the Internet and a very friendly corporate culture. But after a point, even having friends in an unfamiliar place can leave me agitated and prone to impulsive decisions. The simple fact is that there are very few places to go to not be alone at two o'clock in the morning even in New York City. To steal a quote from *The Simpsons*:

> *Insurance adjuster: Err, this place Moe's you left just before the accident—this is a business of some kind?*
>
> *Homer's inner monologue: Don't tell him you were at a bar! But what else is open at night?*
>
> *Homer: It's a pornography store. I was buying pornography.*

Unsurprisingly an agitated state led me to Eighth Avenue in search of something to get away from being alone. Even less surprising is that I ended up at a strip club a few blocks from my hotel.

It was pretty nice as strip clubs go. Seediness seemed to have been kept to a minimum. When not on stage, the dancers circulated on the floor wearing dresses that would be presentable in public. I found a seat in the second row and ordered a drink from the waitress. The stage show was good, and at some point I bought some lap dances. Nothing else really stands out from that night, not due to anything drastic like a blackout, but simply because it was a pleasant but unremarkable experience.

Fast-forward three years.

Another work project brought me back to New York for the first time in a couple of years. Projects move fast at The Company, and each one tends to lead to different travel experiences; in the interim I'd been to Dublin, Sydney, Zurich, and probably more locations lost to memory. It was nice to be back in New York. I booked the same hotel since it had been quite good to me, and it was easy to take the subway to work.

An attentive reader can already see how the next part plays out. Midweek, in the middle of the night and in the middle of a nervous, anxious panic, I headed out onto the streets. I ended up at the same club and sat in the middle row. The waitress brought me a drink as I watched the stage show. The other dancers circulated on the floor, persuading patrons to get lap dances.

And this is when the script changes.

A pretty woman with long dark hair, wearing a floor-length red dress, stopped in front of me, smiled, and said, "I remember you." Then she kept walking and vanished through a door into the mystery that is backstage. She didn't try to sell me a dance. It's not a business where there are slow sales plays.

For someone feeling dangerously disconnected from people, *I remember you* are powerful, compelling words.

She was gone, and I was all but frantic to find her, to find out how and why she remembered me. The doors to the backstage area were obviously barred to the likes of me, and clubs vary in how often the dancers circulate; if one has had a good night otherwise, there might be no reason to work the floor at all. There was a chance she might not come back.

I finished my drink. The ever-attentive cocktail waitress noticed and came over to see if I wanted another.

"Yes, another, please. Also, who was the woman who just went by?"

She gave me a look. "Honey, you're going to have to be way more specific."

"Red dress, long dark hair, just went into the back." I handed her a twenty-dollar bill. "Can you check for me, please?"

The waitress was successful; after a few minutes the mystery woman came back through the door, long hair swinging perfectly as she walked. I smiled in vague recognition, and she sat in the chair next to me. She smiled back. A moment passed. In a state of raw anxiety and probably looking desperately lonely, I managed to get a sentence out.

"Do you really remember me?"

She smiled again and told me a short narrative of our previous meeting. Her account matched everything I remembered and also portrayed me as sweet, polite, and respectful. I was intrigued and flattered, so we repaired to a private booth.

Half an hour later we were sharing a bottle of champagne, she was naked but for a thong, and we were discussing history. I was thrilled to have a pretty girl sitting on my lap, a drink, and an excellent conversation. The situation had all the things I wanted: my prurient interests at least in check, my intellectual faculties fully engaged, and my need for a human connection fulfilled. I was happy.

That was the beginning.

Over the next few years I would see her at least once on every trip to New York. We would text periodically between my trips. After a while, she decided she wouldn't see me at work anymore, and we would meet up for dinner and drinks in a more clothed setting. She would buy me small gifts. I once lent her rent money when she'd had a particularly bad month. She met my then fiancée and some close friends and later attended the New York wedding reception I had after marrying that fiancée. We stayed close.

The last time I saw her was over a long lunch on a Monday afternoon about seven years after we'd first met. I hadn't visited New York for over a year, and we had missed actually seeing another a great deal. We talked for a couple of hours, catching up and being happy. I was in town during the week for work and was staying through the weekend so we could spend more time together. All her weeknights were busy with work, but she had Friday night off, and we made plans to go

see a show together with maybe dinner beforehand. I enthusi-
astically bought our tickets as soon as I got back to the office,
looking forward to an actual date.

On Friday I was excited all morning. Knowing that she
normally slept late to accommodate working nights, I waited
until after lunch to text her about getting dinner before the
show. She didn't reply, and there were no responses to my multiple messages all afternoon. Determined not to let this ruin
my evening, I headed to the theater in the Flatiron District
anyway. She finally replied when I was already in line to get in
that she had one more quick errand to run and would be at the
show after that. The tickets were at will-call under my name,
and I told her that I'd leave hers there, and she'd just need to
give my name at the box office when she got there. I'd wait in
the bar as long as I could.

The show had a strict *no admission* policy once the cur-
tain was raised. I lingered in the bar until the usher gave the
last call. I heard nothing from her. My phone was on silent as
a courtesy to other patrons, but when I got out of the theater
I saw that she still hadn't replied. Walking back to my hotel, I
brooded about the matter. Someone who purported to miss
me a lot for over a year had one chance to really spend time
with me and had put other errands ahead of it. Why? When I
got back to the hotel and still hadn't heard anything I sent her
a message:

> Wish I could've seen you again. I don't under-
> stand what happened but I don't like being
> treated like that. I hope you're okay.

I never heard from her again.

AN IDEAL FOR LIVING

I really don't know how many times I've tried to kill myself, and I'm not sure it can be accurately counted. The minimum count is four serious attempts; the upper limit is much higher. It gets into the complicated issue of suicide versus parasuicide.

For those unfamiliar, *parasuicide* is a blanket term for engaging in self-harm that is similar to a suicide attempt or deliberate, risky behaviors that can lead indirectly to death. Professional opinions differ on whether said behaviors are intended to get attention. In most cases it's very clearly one way or the other. Overall, mine were definitely not seeking attention; I went to great measures to keep them secret, cutting in places where no one would see. This is remarkably easy when no one is paying a lot of attention. Many of these acts are easily classified as parasuicide. As a former therapist of mine once pointed out, "No one who owns a gun tries to kill themselves with a razor blade."

It wasn't always covert. At one point in high school I gave up even pretending to hide it. I always sat in the back row of my junior year English class. I'd hold a razor blade on my tongue for the entire hour, and I was daring everyone to say anything. One day I spat the blade out and started carving into my arm.

A girl in my class, barely an acquaintance and certainly not a friend, noticed and called me out on it in a whisper.

"Gus! Gus! What are you doing?"

I didn't have an answer. The razor was about a quarter inch deep in my forearm, and I was trying to pull it forward. Even with a fresh razor blade, flesh does not cut easily.

"If you don't go to the nurse right now I'm telling Mrs. Johnson what you're doing."

No one had ever called me out like that. Not family, not friends, not professionals. A girl I wasn't friends with called me on it. I dropped the bloody razor blade and ran out of the classroom holding my bleeding forearm. I couldn't see anything in my blind panic. I went to the nurse, who for her own reasons had been turning a blind eye for years.

More of a gray area is the first time I attempted suicide by slitting my left wrist. I'd already been cutting for nearly a decade without suicidal intent. The scars are still visible in the right light, but none of the cuts were deep enough to actually hit the artery. Still, they bled, and I crouched over a sink full of warm water to keep them from closing before I passed out. Legitimate attempt, poor execution. Does that count? It was a sincere attempt by a scared adolescent. It just happened not to be fatal.

Confirmed attempt number two: I got stopped, by accident, at eighteen. I was working as a counselor at a Boy Scout summer camp, and I'd gathered enough over-the-counter sleep aids over the course of a few weeks to probably at least down me for a bit. I had them sitting in a pile on the desk with a glass of orange juice when a random accident brought my manager back into the commissary. She'd been a good boss and was the mother of a friend. She trashed the pills and asked her husband, John, another volunteer at camp, to talk to me.

The timeless actor Peter Boyle described his role in *Taxi Driver* as trying to talk hope to someone who's past hearing it.

John tried to explain to me that everybody is down sometimes, including several Scout leaders we knew who were veterans with PTSD, as well as my ex-girlfriend, who'd recently lost her mother to cancer. My *secret* ex-girlfriend who didn't want anyone to know we had dated, that is. Unsurprisingly the talk didn't help. I do believe that John and Donna did everything they could.

Five hours later I tried again with a combination of ice packs, razor blades, and crying. I got close. The dark color of the blood and the pulsing flow meant I'd hit the artery. I don't remember how many stitches it took to close it. I do remember losing my nerve, applying pressure with a towel, and running to find a friend to ask for help. I woke up in the county hospital.

Compare and contrast: slicing open my ulnar artery at eighteen counts as a suicide attempt; holding an unloaded revolver to my temple at twenty-five just to feel the cold muzzle does not. I wanted to be comfortable with the muzzle touching me. After all, if you're going to shoot yourself, dying is far better than ending up vegetative or in a coma. Most people who attempt suicide by gunshot flinch. Best of a bad situation. I'm nothing if not pragmatic.

Leaving self-harm aside, how many choices were deliberate attempts to make something bad happen? Enough lack of self-interest and one wanders down surprising paths, a lot of them pretty bad. Goading drivers who are cavalier about crosswalks. Walking home drunk through bad neighborhoods. Carrying a gun to see what might happen. Verbally provoking people to try to get them to throw the first punch. Casually mixing pills and alcohol. I've done all these things.

I remember trying to hit my femoral artery with a razor blade when I was twenty-four. The scars are still pretty ugly, but I didn't make it. Lying on my bathroom floor, crying and bleeding, I blacked out. I was disappointed that I awoke. Despite what people think about cats, The Admiral was more concerned with trying to wake me than lapping up the puddle of blood pooled on the floor. He pawed at my face, his paws wet with my blood. "Meow? Meow?" I woke up and cried. Later I cleaned up the blood. Not hard to do on cheap vinyl flooring.

I decided to live. It was a harder decision than you think.

The self-destructive urge still comes up occasionally. The worst times are actually watching what most people think of as heroic deaths in media. In the calculus of death, it's not suicide if you die to save someone else. It's not suicide if you fall on the grenade or take the bullet to save someone. It's not suicide if you intervene to help someone being attacked. It's not suicide even when you make a bad, dangerous choice, as long as it is to help someone else. I cry openly watching every one of those fictional deaths. To people with a history of suicide attempts, the proverbial "good death" is incredibly compelling. It assuages the guilt about the selfishness of suicide by assigning it a higher purpose. Psychologists call this passive suicidal ideation, and in some situations it is more dangerous than active suicidal ideation.

That's it. There really isn't an ending here, which is kind of the point.

ABOUT THE AUTHOR

A Hartmann is a systems engineer for a major Internet firm and resides in Seattle. This is his first book.